THE WORLD OF
HARLEY-DAVIDSON

THE WORLD OF
HARLEY-DAVIDSON

EXPLORING THE LEGEND OF AN AMERICAN DREAM

MAC McDIARMID

southwater

This edition is published by Southwater, an imprint of Anness Publishing Ltd,
Hermes House, 88–89 Blackfriars Road, London SE1 8HA; tel. 020 7401 2077; fax 020 7633 9499

www.southwaterbooks.com; www.annesspublishing.com

Anness Publishing has a new picture agency outlet for images for publishing, promotions or advertising.
Please visit our website www.practicalpictures.com for more information.

UK agent: The Manning Partnership Ltd; tel. 01225 478444; fax 01225 478440;
sales@manning-partnership.co.uk
UK distributor: Grantham Book Services Ltd; tel. 01476 541080;
fax 01476 541061; orders@gbs.tbs-ltd.co.uk
North American agent/distributor: National Book Network;
tel. 301 459 3366; fax 301 429 5746; www.nbnbooks.com
Australian agent/distributor: Pan Macmillan Australia;
tel. 1300 135 113; fax 1300 135 103; customer.service@macmillan.com.au
New Zealand agent/distributor: David Bateman Ltd;
tel. (09) 415 7664; fax (09) 415 8892

© Anness Publishing Ltd 2003, 2008

A CIP catalogue record for this book is available from the British Library.

Publisher Joanna Lorenz
Managing Editor Judith Simons
Project Editor Mariano Kälfors
Designer Mike Morey
Production Controller Claire Rae

Previously published as part of a larger compendium, *Harley Davidson: A Visual History*

Publisher's note
In recognition of the uniquely American pedigree of the motorcycles featured on the following pages, engine
capacity is generally expressed in imperial units (cubic inches) with the metric equivalent (cc) in brackets.
However, even Harley-Davidson employ units somewhat arbitrarily, favouring cu in for heavyweight twins, but
ccs for Sportster models, a practice we have also adopted.
The capacity of Harley engines should also be treated with some care. Even from the early days, the inch sizes
quoted and used by Harley fans were a sort of numeric shorthand, relating only approximately to measured
reality. More recently, even the "80-inch" Evo engine actually measured 81.8cu in – a difference of no less
than 29cc. In general, where an engine is referred to as something-inch, this refers to popular usage.
Dimensions expressed in cu in and/or cc are as accurate as records permit.
We trust that this historical ambiguity will not reduce the reader's enjoyment.

CONTENTS

THE WORLD OF HARLEY-DAVIDSON

"If you have to ask…" said the Harley-Davidson slogan, "…you wouldn't understand." Just what is it that makes Harley-Davidson so special? The company makes motorcycles, true, but it is much more than a mere motorcycle manufacturer – Milwaukee makes legends. The company that has become an American icon crafts heavy metal into love affairs, forges lifestyles and fulfils dreams. As much myth as motorcycle – often imitated, never copied – there is simply nothing quite like a Harley-Davidson.

Today, Harleys are as recognizable around the world as the Stars and Stripes, as ubiquitous as McDonald's and as prized for their rugged honesty as Zippo lighters and Levi's. They appear in movies and advertising; they're the wheels of choice for celebrities and stars. Elvis owned one and, according to the T-shirt at least, God rides one too. Men have raced them almost as soon as the first one came out of the shop. They have been a unique facet of American life through two world wars and a crippling Depression.

Harley-Davidson's is the longest history in motorcycling, almost the story of motorcycling itself, and *The World of Harley-Davidson* is the epic tale of the making of an American legend.

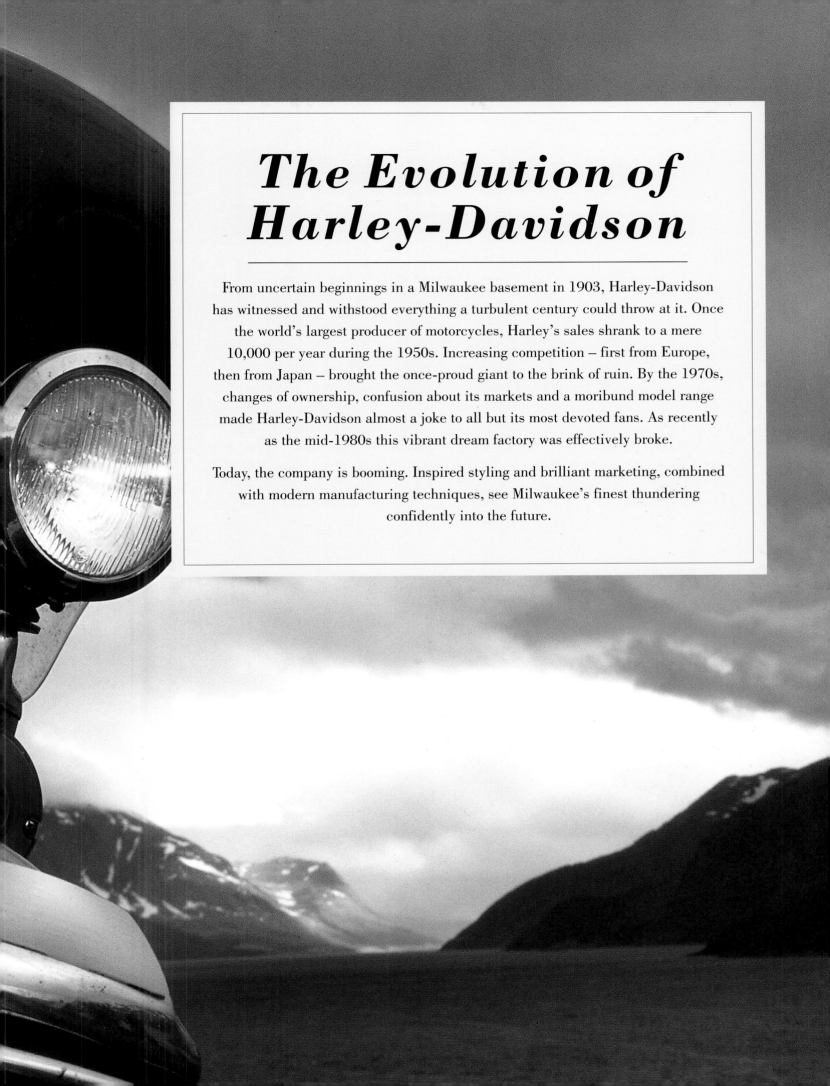

The Evolution of Harley-Davidson

From uncertain beginnings in a Milwaukee basement in 1903, Harley-Davidson has witnessed and withstood everything a turbulent century could throw at it. Once the world's largest producer of motorcycles, Harley's sales shrank to a mere 10,000 per year during the 1950s. Increasing competition – first from Europe, then from Japan – brought the once-proud giant to the brink of ruin. By the 1970s, changes of ownership, confusion about its markets and a moribund model range made Harley-Davidson almost a joke to all but its most devoted fans. As recently as the mid-1980s this vibrant dream factory was effectively broke.

Today, the company is booming. Inspired styling and brilliant marketing, combined with modern manufacturing techniques, see Milwaukee's finest thundering confidently into the future.

EARLY YEARS

In the early days of the 20th century, young men in dingy workshops across the industrialized world tinkered with an endless array of new-fangled mechanical contraptions. There may have been hundreds of such enthusiastic amateurs in Wisconsin alone, but it was the relatively untutored tinkering of two young Milwaukee men in particular that would give rise to an American legend.

The story begins in 1900 – 15 years after Gottlieb Daimler created the world's first powered two-wheeler and only six years after the first production machine – when William Sylvester Harley and Arthur Davidson got together in a Milwaukee basement with motorcycling in mind.

Information from these early years is sketchy, so the inspiration for their enthusiasm is unclear. A primitive motorcycle was demonstrated by its creator, Edward Joel Pennington, on nearby Wisconsin Avenue as early as 1895, though it's not clear whether the duo actually witnessed the event. They are known to have been impressed by a variety act five years later, however, in which comedienne Anna Held rode a French-built motorcycle across the stage of Milwaukee's Bijou theatre.

Harley was just 20 at the time, Davidson a year younger. The pair had been friends since their school days and, by accident or fate, had already accumulated some of the skills their

■ ABOVE *The founders, from left: Arthur Davidson, Walter Davidson, William Harley and William Davidson.*

■ BELOW *What is believed to be the very first production Harley-Davidson, now fully restored, enjoys pride of place in the Juneau Avenue lobby.*

■ RIGHT AND BELOW
The Model 5D twin from
1909 was essentially
two singles on a
common crankcase.
Valve gear problems
meant that only 27
were built. Production
of an improved version
began for 1911 with
the Model 7D.

■ RIGHT *America's*
early road network was
primitive, but
motorcycles proved
easier to manhandle
than cars.

dreams required by the time they began working together in that Milwaukee basement. Harley worked as a draughtsman and had six years of experience in bicycle manufacturing; Davidson was a pattern maker with the same company as Harley, working on small petrol (gas) engines. They were also fortunate enough to have working alongside them a German colleague familiar with pioneering European motorcycles. Work on the first Harley-Davidson engine began in 1900 or 1901 and was probably based on one of the do-it-yourself kits then available, itself roughly based on the French De Dion-Bouton design. A drawing dated 20 July 1901 shows a 7.07cu in (115.8cc) engine with a bore and stroke of 2 x 2.25in (50 x 55mm). When installed in a bicycle, power proved deeply disappointing.

At least one more prototype followed, including a machine capable of "thrilling speeds up to 25mph" and measuring 10.2cu in (167cc). It soon became clear that their venture required more expertise if it was ever going to get up to speed – beginning with the need for a skilled mechanic. Fortunately, Arthur's brother, Walter Davidson, was just such a man.

Walter was working as a railroad machinist in Parsons, Kansas, at the time, but was due in Milwaukee for the wedding of a third Davidson brother, William A. (Bill). Arthur wrote to Walter, offering him a ride on their new motorcycle. It was only later that he discovered ("imagine my chagrin") that he would have to help build it first. He must have liked the idea though –, enough to find work in Milwaukee and join the team. The founders became four when William, the eldest Davidson brother and a foreman railway toolmaker, jumped on board – and the four began the ride of their lives.

The machine recognized as the first true Harley-Davidson engine was built during 1902-3, by which time locally built Merkel and Mitchell motorcycles were already a familiar feature of Milwaukee life. Bore and stroke were 3 x 3.5in (76.2 x 88.9mm) for a displacement of 24.74cu in (405cc) but the Harley-Davidson engine incorporated many technical refinements. The new engine was of F-head layout, with much larger cooling fins than before, as well as much larger flywheels – almost 10in (250mm) across. Some of the machining was done on a lathe belonging to a friend, Henry Melk, while other parts were crafted illicitly as parts for foreign sales in the toolrooms of William A. Davidson's employers, the Chicago, Milwaukee and St Paul Railroad. Legend has it that the first carburettor was made from a discarded tomato can (although this could as easily refer to the 1901 engine), and Bill Harley later described its spark plug, which had cost the princely sum of $3.00, as being "as big as a doorknob".

■ ABOVE *By 1913 all Harley twins enjoyed all-chain drive, although the basic Model 9A single (right) continued with leather belt drive.*

■ BELOW *A well-to-do couple with a Model 9A, pictured in 1913.*

Assistance with the design came from Arthur's childhood friend, Ole Evinrude, who was already making liquid-cooled engines of his own and would later find fame with his outboard motors. Evinrude is credited with setting up the carburettor, but other components – notably the roller tappets still used on Harleys today – may have been his idea as well. Scaling 49lbs (22kg), this engine was installed in a loop frame similar to the existing Merkel design, in the Davidson family's back yard at 315 37th Street. The site, known as 38th Street today, is now owned by the giant Miller Brewery and is little more than a stone's throw from Juneau Avenue.

■ THE HARLEY-DAVIDSON MOTOR CO.

So it was that in 1903 – the same year the Wright brothers took to the air – the Harley-Davidson team created its first motorcycle and readied itself to produce similar machines for public consumption. This handsome machine was gloss black with gold pinstriping, a single-loop tubular steel frame, unsprung forks and leather belt final drive directly from the crankshaft. Additional power was offered by pedals, which also provided the only braking force. It is unclear how many machines were built during 1904 – sources suggest figures anywhere from one to eight, although anything over three seems unlikely. However many there were, each was assembled in a 15 x 10ft shed erected in the Davidson back yard by the boys' father, a cabinet-maker. Modest though it was, the shed bore the legend "Harley-Davidson

■ BELOW *This celebratory restoration of a 1913 single shows an image of the first factory (which was located on Juneau Avenue, Milwaukee) on the tank.*

Motor Co." on its front (and only) door with typical understated pride.

The first production Harley has a tale to tell all its own. It carried its first owner, a Mr Mayer, for almost 6,000 miles before passing to George Lyon, who covered another 15,000 miles. It was sold in turn to a Dr Webster, followed by Louis Fluke and Stephen Sparrow, who between them clocked up almost another 62,000 relatively untroubled miles (a total of 134,000 km). By 1913, the company decided to advertise the bike's exploits, promoting an image of dependable travel:

■ ABOVE *The inlet-over-exhaust valve layout is clearly seen on this early "Renault Gray" single.*

■ LEFT *William S. Harley on the left and Walter Davidson on the right getting a motorcycle over the rocks of a creek, 1912.*

"100,000 miles on its original bearings and no major components replaced". Harley-Davidson engines were also produced for use in "buckboards" (four-wheel wagons) and the company's earliest advertisements also proposed their use in boats.

Motorcycle production soared to seven in 1905 as the company took on its first outside employee and attracted its first dealer, C.H. Lang of Chicago, who would become the largest motorcycle dealer in the country within a dozen years. A year later, in 1906, "Renault gray with red pinstriping" joined black as a colour option, and the model became known as "the Silent Gray Fellow", a name that reflected its quietness and dependability.

Engine capacity had by now increased to 26.84cu in (440cc) and the list price for the latest models was $200.

Production had soared to 50 units by 1906, prompting a move from the company's original hut on 37th Street and Highway Boulevard into its first proper building on the present Juneau Avenue site. The new factory turned out to be sitting partially on land belonging to the railroad. Fortunately, the "factory" was a wooden structure, and at 28 x 80ft (9 x 25 metres) eight or ten people were able to carry it the few feet to its proper location.

Finance for expansion came from a relative, James McLay, known as "the honey uncle" due to his generosity and hobby of beekeeping. This affectionate tribute was more appropriate than anyone could imagine, for Juneau Avenue was to become a veritable hive of activity, seven days a week, 365 days a year.

■ FORGING AHEAD

By 1907, the company was getting serious: it became Harley-Davidson Inc. Walter was the largest stockholder, followed by Arthur, with the two Williams a joint third. A Davidson sister, Elizabeth, also had the good sense to buy Harley-Davidson shares early in the firm's

■ BELOW RIGHT AND LEFT *An unrestored and original 1915 61-inch F-head twin. Note that pedal assistance is still retained.*

■ ABOVE *A rare 1914 Model 10C single with hugely complex two-speed rear hub.*

■ BELOW *Harley-Davidson motorcycles and sidecars were used by the rural postal service.*

life. (By 1916, Davidson family stockholders would outnumber Harleys seventeen to three.) It was a heady time. The company had already taken on extra staff; William Harley had begun an engineering degree at the University of Wisconsin in Madison; Walter was exploring the mysteries of heat treatment on metals; and the enterprise, and Arthur, as company secretary and sales manager, was taking a more

professional approach to production and training. The company may have begun as four young men with more enthusiasm than talent, but they had ambitions for the company they had created. That year, they produced no fewer than 150 machines and within 12 months had sold the first of many thousands for police duty.

Even so, it was clear that further progress demanded a more ambitious new motorcycle than the existing single, which in 1909 expanded to 30.17cu in (495cc). By 1908, William Harley had graduated and continued work on a more potent engine. This bore fruit a year later with the launch of the company's first production V-twin, the Model D, essentially a doubled-up single with strengthened bottom-end.

The first such model became officially available on 15 February 1909, although the first working prototype appears to have been built as early as 1906. A press report from the time clearly mentions a 53in (869cc) Harley twin in April 1908, while a privately-owned Harley-Davidson twin won a hill climb event at Algonquin, Illinois, in July that same year.

Whatever its exact development history, the Model D twin was an inlet-over-exhaust valve design with a capacity of 53.7cu in (880cc), developing around six horsepower and capable

■ LEFT *By 1917 Olive Green had replaced Renault Gray as the factory colour, here on a Model J twin three-speed.*

The factory resisted official racing for several years despite widespread success in competitions. The factory's reluctance continued even when a private owner took the new 61in (989cc) X8E twin (the first Harley with a clutch) to victory in the 1912 San José road race by no less than 17 miles (27km): Bill Harley established a works race department two years later.

of a top speed close to 62mph (100 kph). The cylinders were splayed apart at the trademark 45 degree angle.

The strength of the Model D twin was amply proven in June 1908 when Walter drove one of his bikes to its first "official" competition success, a two-day endurance run in New York's Catskill Mountains. The sole Harley scored a "perfect" 1,000 points, outstripping all the more fancied runners in a field of 61 machines. Surprisingly – and embarrassingly – the first production twins were beset by valve-gear problems, with production being suspended during 1910.

■ BELOW LEFT *Since opening in 1919, this Juneau Avenue factory has been the home of Harley-Davidson.*

■ BELOW RIGHT *William Ottaway, who was Harley's first race boss, sits astride a 1924 Model JDCA.*

■ A DEPENDABLE TWIN

When the V-engine reappeared as the "50-inch" (810cc) Model 7D of 1911, no expense had been spared and every effort made to produce a machine worthy of Harley-Davidson's reputation. Not only had proper mechanical valves replaced the hit-and-miss automatic inlets, an adjustable tensioner had been added to the slippage-prone belt final drive.

Another notable improvement to this model saw the revised powerplant housed in a new, much sturdier frame.

■ RIGHT *Gordon, Walter Jnr. and Allan Davidson (sitting on bikes) in San Francisco after a cross-country ride in 1929.*

A year later, a 61cu in (989cc) version, the chain-drive Model X8E, reinforced these developments. With its second attempt, Harley hit the nail on the head, and the V-twin took its rightful place in Milwaukee history.

Production in the rapidly expanding company soared to 450 machines in 1908, housed in a new, brick-built factory of

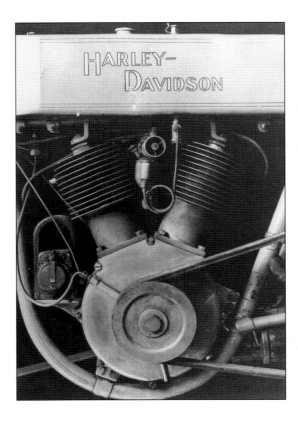

■ RIGHT *Harley-Davidson's first V-Twin engine, introduced in 1909. It displaced 49.5cu in (811cc).*

2,380sq ft (221sq metres) and employing 18 people. New machinery arrived almost weekly and was set to work, according to legend, "as soon as the cement was dry", and in what must have seemed like an instant, became obsolete. Two years later, 149 staff were engaged in another new factory – a reinforced concrete structure of 9,520sq ft (885sq metres).

By the time the new 5hp, 35cu in single model (565cc 5–35) appeared in 1913, the company had established a reputation for producing machines that were dependable in both domestic and competitive use. The factory was hurtling ahead as well in this changing age and included a separate Parts and Accessories Department. More than 1,500 employees worked for a company whose manufacturing floor area had grown from nothing to almost 300,000sq ft (28,000sq metres) within a decade. Production rocketed from eight machines in 1905 to 1,149 in 1911 and 17,439 in 1916, the year prior to the United States' entry into the First World War.

Though not yet dominant in the industry, in 1913 Harley produced around 18 per cent of the 70,000 American-built motorcycles.

Very soon, however, all this would change, and much of this energy would be called to the service of Uncle Sam.

WAR AND PEACE

On 6 April 1917, the United States declared war on Germany. Harley's successful peace-time formula suddenly faced an entirely new set of demands for which, five years earlier, the company may have been ill-prepared. By 1917, however, this bullish, expanding company was ready to go to war for real.

Harley-Davidson supplied the best part of 20,000 motorcycles to the American military in total, the majority being 61-inch twins. Indeed, the war did little but good for the company's prospects. Rival European motorcycle manufacturers were preoccupied by hostilities for a much longer period (1914–18) than those in the United States. Consequently, Milwaukee was able to extend its markets and reputation overseas. By 1918, aided by a $3 million loan from the M&I bank, Harley-Davidson had

become the world's largest manufacturer of motorcycles. Within a year, "Hap" Scherer had been appointed Harley-Davidson's first publicity manager. By 1921, machines were being sold through 2,000 dealers in 67 countries, with product catalogues printed in seven languages. As the dust settled on the carnage of the war, one-sixth of Milwaukee's production was destined for export.

■ ABOVE *Harley was quick to develop its bikes for war, including mounting them with machine guns.*

■ BELOW *Milwaukee-built sidecars proved to be extremely popular for both military and civilian use.*

■ RIGHT *Board racers were Harleys in their leanest form, stripped of even any semblance of brakes...*

The aftermath of war had other, less predictable side-effects. One of these was the retention of army green as the company colour in place of the pre-war pale grey. Another more enduring effect concerned training. To help military personnel keep Milwaukee's wares reliable, the Harley-Davidson Service School was established in 1917. Initially intended as a military measure and as concerned with riding instruction as mechanics, the Service School soon developed into a crucial arm of the factory's civilian service.

By the eve of the "Roaring Twenties", the Juneau Avenue factory had become a colossus. In 1919, close to 1,800 employees toiled on a floor area exceeding 400,000sq ft (37,000sq metres) to produce 22,685 motorcycles and

■ RIGHT *...or silencing, as can clearly be seen on this handsome 1916 F-head twin.*

■ BELOW *Front brakes finally arrived in the late 1920s, as on this Model J Big Twin.*

over 16,000 sidecars. The Model J Sport Twin, unveiled that same year, was unique among Harleys, if not American motorcycles in general. Instead of the "V" layout, the 35.6cu in (584cc) twin adopted a horizontally opposed design, akin to today's BMWs. Instead of lying across the frame, the cylinders were orientated fore-and-aft. Although long and unwieldy, the layout offered a very low centre of gravity and a compact width, ideally suited to America's then-primitive road network.

There were other innovations, most of which would stand the test of time better than the model itself. The final drive was sensibly protected from dust in a metal enclosure, not unlike more recent MZ machines, lubricated by oil mist from the engine breather. It was also the first model to feature a full electrical system produced by the Harley factory. Although the Sport set many records – Canada to Mexico in less than 75 hours, no easy task even today – its six horsepower engine lacked the bottomless big-inch power America demanded, and was discontinued after 1922.

The 1920s didn't so much roar as whimper where motorcycles were concerned. Much of the blame for the Sport Twin's relative failure lay far beyond Milwaukee's control – 1920

■ BELOW *Inventiveness is apparent in this 1919 twin, fitted with stabilising skis for use in icy conditions.*

witnessed a major trade recession with a massive over-supply of manufactured goods as global economies struggled to adjust to peace-time trade. One of the consequences was Henry Ford's slashing the price of his Model T car to $395, the same as the biggest Harley twin. The effects on motorcycle sales were inevitable. The trade slump was brief, but America's love affair with the car was not, and neither Harley nor any other bike manufacturer fully recovered their previous momentum.

Milwaukee's sales collapsed from over 28,000 in 1920 to 10,202 in 1921, with sales so poor during that spring that the factory, which had expanded 12 months before, shut down for a month. Sales would not return to 1920s levels for a further 21 years. Most of the machines that were sold during that time were 61-inch V-twins.

Although the Sport failed to make the impact Harley hoped, one of the next models quickly became a Milwaukee legend. In 1921, the V-twin was replaced by the JD and FD, the first 74-inch (actually 74.2cu in/1,216cc) models, with F-head, inlet-over-exhaust (ioe) valve layout. Each example was dubbed a "Superpowered Twin" in tribute to its 18-hp engine and both underwent rigorous pre-delivery testing: yet another Harley innovation.

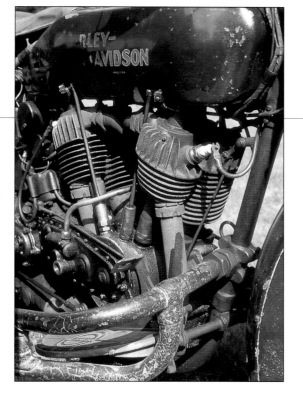

■ RIGHT *The 1920s was marked mostly by F-head machines like this 1922 61-inch twin. Flatheads began to appear from 1926, the same year as the first overhead valve engines.*

As for the rest of the range, the 30-inch single had been dropped after 1918. In 1926, a new single – the 21in (344cc) Model A – was introduced, joined four years later by a 30.5in (492cc) sister. In a radical move, Harley-Davidson pioneered the front brake in 1928, just as the company had pioneered kick-starts and three-speed transmissions more than a decade earlier. All models were sold in varied specifications of transmission, valve-gear and power, so that in 1928, for instance, three basic

engine types accounted for no less than a dozen models. By this time, Harley's only surviving domestic competitors were Indian, Henderson, Cleveland and Super-X.

The last year of the decade introduced the machine that would become Milwaukee's bread and butter. The new WL was a 45in (742cc) side-valve V-twin which supposedly combined the single's agility with the power of the bigger twins. Capped by rakish twin "bullet" headlights, the new model was an instant success and constituted the lowest rung on a V-twin ladder made up of 45-, 61- and 74-inchers). Star billing in the 1929 Harley-Davidson catalogue went to the JDH Two-Cam, which housed a specially-prepared variant of the 74-inch engine that had been developed for the factory's all-conquering board racers.

Billed as "the fastest road model that Harley-Davidson has ever offered to the public", it could probably out-run any other two-wheeler on the American highway.

The WL may have been humbler but it proved its worth by keeping Milwaukee's head above water in the years ahead.

■ RIGHT *This stylish ohv "Peashooter" speedway machine dates from 1927.*

THE 1930s

The 1930s began in high spirits with arguably the most mouth-watering range to come out of Milwaukee for years. All models now had bigger brakes and tyres, improved ground clearance, lower saddles and – best of all – removable cylinder heads. These "Ricardo" heads were far more practical and efficient than the one-piece iron cylinders previously employed. Although plagued by early problems, the new high-compression 74.2cu in (1,216cc) VL offered fully 15 per cent more power than any previous Harley roadster. A nation-wide "open house" attracted customers by the thousands and, with sales quickly up 30 per cent on the previous year, the new decade appeared rich in promise.

There was one cloud on the horizon, however. In October 1929, a few weeks after the 1930 range was unveiled, the Wall Street stock market crashed, sending tremors throughout the American economy and the rest of the world. President Herbert Hoover's initial rapid intervention seemed to stem the tide but economic confidence continued to wilt. In 1930, 1,300 banks went to the wall. Manufacturers in every industry offered incentives to stimulate business, but to no avail. Within 12 months, the mighty Juneau Avenue factory was running at a mere 10 per cent of production capacity and would report a loss of more than $320,000 the following year. By 1933, one quarter of the United States workforce was unemployed. Few people had

■ ABOVE *By the 1930s all Harleys were flatheads, such as this imposing 74-inch VL from 1933.*

■ LEFT *1932 saw the introduction of the enduring Servi-Car, which would continue in production for 40 years.*

■ ABOVE *The troubles of the Depression encouraged novel art-deco styling, such as the tank badge on this mammoth 80-inch VLH from 1936. The same motifs can be seen even on modern Harleys.*

money to spend on motorcycles. Of hundreds of American bike manufacturers, only Harley and Indian had the financial strength and acumen to survive. Industry-wide production fell from 32,000 to 6,000 units per year by 1933, by which time fewer than 100,000 motorcycles were registered in the whole of the United States. Of these new sales, Milwaukee's share was just 3,703 – its lowest in 23 years.

Desperately, Juneau Avenue wracked its brains for innovative sales ideas, ranging from savings plans to a medal scheme intended to turn every Harley owner into a salesman. One enduring response was the sale of branded clothing and accessories – a sideline now worth millions of dollars per year. A superficial but significant measure was the abandonment of dull green paint in 1933, in favour of more vivid colours and art-deco graphics which continue to brighten Harley-Davidsons today.

An altogether grittier response was the three-wheeled Servi-Car, a cheap delivery and police

vehicle powered by the 45-inch (742cc) Model D engine. Surprisingly, given the fraught circumstances of the time, this three-wheeler was both a sound design and a solid piece of engineering – so tough and enduring, indeed, that it survived in production from late 1931 until 1974. The true hero of the Depression years was the side-valve twin: cheap to produce, economic to run and maintain, and easily repairable.

Almost on their own, the D and V models saw Harley through the Depression, along with the 30.5in (492cc) single-cylinder machine of 1929. As the financial vice tightened, no other significant new models were developed during those six years.

In many ways, the worst of the Depression also brought out the best in the company. By reducing the length of the working week, as many staff were kept on as possible, although this was less generous than it might appear, since it was partially mandated by the government's National Recovery Administration, and every skilled hand would be needed when the slump finally abated. Prudent financial controls, police and military contracts, novel sales strategies and energetic pursuit of exports kept the company afloat, and by 1934, the books were back in the black.

■ KNUCKLING DOWN

Painfully slowly, President Roosevelt's "New Deal" began to take effect and, by 1936, the

■ ABOVE LEFT *A WLA in desert camouflage stands out against civilian chrome.*

ABOVE RIGHT AND BELOW *Drab green was more common. Almost 90,000 of these 45-inch (742cc) flathead twins were built for the military during the Second World War, and thousands served with the Soviet forces.*

crippling Depression came to a close. New machines began to emerge from Milwaukee, whose 1935 model range had comprised a mere two basic models. These were the 45-inch (742cc) Model R (essentially the D model with light alloy pistons, soon to become the heroic W) and the 74-inch (1,216cc) Model V and its derivatives, now cured of its original and varied ills. Both were side-valve designs, slow and steady, whereas the American public increasingly craved more advanced machines.

The biggest newcomer was the V-twin Model UL. Although still side-valve and visually similar to the proven DL45, it displaced a stupendous 78.9cu in (1,293cc), making it ideal for heavy sidecar use. It was to continue in production until 1945. Most important of all was a new generation of 61-inch (898cc) twin with overhead valves and twice the power of its predecessor. The legendary Model E – the Knucklehead – had arrived.

The 1936 Knuckle could have appeared in 1934 but for government restrictions aimed at reducing employment. For company and public alike, this was frustrating but certainly worth the wait. The Knuckle was a Juneau Avenue first in many respects – the first four (forward)

■ **ABOVE LEFT AND RIGHT** *The "A" in WLA stood for army, so naturally military rules came with the machines. Soldiers were warned not to exceed 65mph.*

■ **RIGHT AND BELOW** *Even soldiers could be customizers: note the "Uncle Sam" on the fuel tank (right) and grenade-box lettering (below).*

speeder; the first overhead valve roadster twin; the first hemispherical heads. The engine was heavily influenced by the competition experience of the legendary Joe Petrali, Harley development rider and near-unbeatable racer. It announced its arrival by 136.183mph (219.16kph) on the sands of Daytona Beach, Florida. The rider, naturally, was Joe. His waterside speed record stands to this day.

With the new model as its flagship, Harley's fortunes rapidly improved. In 1937, sales exceeded 11,000 for the first time since 1930. The same year brought significant improvements elsewhere in the range: full roller bearing engines, chromolly fork tubes and interchangeable wheels.

As well as these technical advances, the lessons of the Depression had instilled in the company a faith in styling and cosmetics which

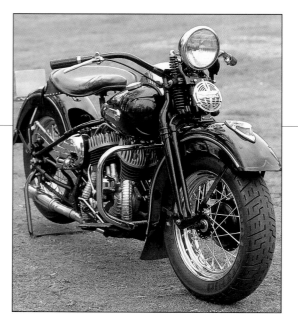

stands them in good stead even today. The aftermarket and art-deco innovations of 1932 were continued. Balloon tyres appeared in 1940 (more striking, if less functional, than new aluminium alloy heads for the flathead side-valve models). In 1941, four-speed transmissions became standard across the big twin range. Eleven models were now on the books in four basic engine configurations: side-valves of 45-, 74- and 80-inch (742, 1,216 and 1,293cc), and Knuckleheads of 61-inch Model E (989cc) and 74-inch Model F (1,207cc).

■ BACK TO WAR

Motorcycle production in Milwaukee rose from a low of 3,703 in 1933 to more than 18,000 in 1941. Harley made it through the Depression by the narrowest of squeaks, emerging stronger than ever before. However, not long after this rocky period in Harley-Davidson's history, a catastrophe of an altogether more terrible kind occurred: the world once again went to war.

The United States entered the conflict after the bombing of Pearl Harbor on 7 December 1941.

As the country's largest motorcycle producer, it fell to Harley-Davidson to underpin the bulk of the country's two-wheeled war effort. Throughout the years of America's involvement in the war (1942–45), practically the entire output of the Milwaukee factory was turned over to military production – some 90,000 machines in total.

As with the First World War, the Second was fairly good to Milwaukee. In 1940, sales

■ LEFT *During the Second World War almost no machines were made for civilian use. This is one of the first post-war WL45 twins, in vibrant red.*

totalled less than 11,000. These soared to 18,000 as the military build-up began in 1941, reaching more than 29,000 in each of the two years that followed before tailing off again as peace approached. However, since the military favoured Harley Davidson's robust side-valve plodders over the new Model E and Model F, this meant that Knucklehead production was practically zero during the same period.

■ RIGHT *The noble Knucklehead, Milwaukee's first overhead valve roadster twin.*

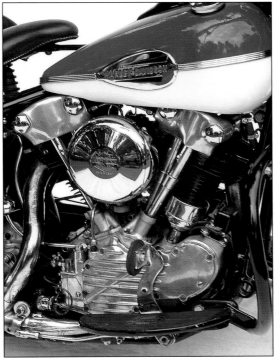

HARLEY JAPAN

One little-known, highly ironic consequence of Milwaukee's quest for export markets in the 1920s and the economic slump of the 1930s was the creation of a Japanese big twin. During the 1920s, Arthur Davidson had pursued new sales openings with vigour, including the establishment of the Harley-Davidson Sales Company of Japan with a comprehensive network of dealers, agencies and spares distributors. Milwaukee's stock stood so high that Harleys soon became Japan's official police motorcycle.

Less worthily, in 1924 the Murata Iron Works began building copies of the 1922 Model J, but the quality was appalling. Murata would later build the Meguro, a distant precursor of modern Kawasakis. Harley exports to Japan all but ceased in the wake of the 1929 Wall Street crash, as the global economic slump crippled the yen. The story might have stopped there but for Alfred Childs, head of Harley's Japanese operation, who asked: "Why not build Harleys there?"

Juneau Avenue was sceptical at first, but such was Childs' persistence that Harley's first overseas factory soon began production at Shinagawa, near Tokyo. Built with tooling, plans, blueprints and expertise borrowed from Milwaukee, the factory was considered the most modern in the world. By 1935 Shinagawa was manufacturing complete motorcycles, mainly 74-inch V-series flathead twins. In 1930, these had become the official motorcycle of the Japanese Imperial Army. Later, when the army became the effective civil power, it declined the chance to convert production to the new ohv Knucklehead, preferring the proven durability of the side-valve twin. It was at this point that the Sankyo corporation took over control of the factory and began selling Japanese Harleys under the Rikuo name. The "74" twin became the Rikuo Model 97.

As an increasingly truculent Japan readied for war, Harley cut its losses and sold out. As military demand increased (especially after the invasion of China in 1937), Rikuo sub-licensed the product to Nihon Jidosha ("Japan Combustion Equipment Co."). Its "Harleys" were variants of the model 97s, entitled Kuro Hagane ("Black Iron").

Ominously, the factory had only a few more years to run. Nihon Jidosha was located in Hiroshima.

BACK TO PEACE

Although the Second World War ended on 15 August 1945 following the Japanese surrender, it would be more than a year before the unveiling of any new revisions from Milwaukee. Even these – theoretically 1947 models – were no more than cosmetic updates of Harley's pre-war machines. Of all the changes, perhaps the best remembered is Brook Steven's design for new "streamlined" H-D tank badges. A revamped clothing and accessories catalogue appeared in the same model year, a harbinger of the direction the company would take three decades later.

For the time being, however, motorcycles were scarce as the industry readjusted to civilian production and the loss of military demand. In the aftermath of the War Department's cancellation of orders for over 11,000 machines in 1944, more than 500 Harley-Davidson workers were let go. The rest, limited to a shortened working week, went on strike in late 1945. Paradoxically, limits on civilian production remained in force, and

■ BELOW *But by 1948 the Knucklehead was history as the era of the Panhead had begun, as with this HydraGlide.*

things went from bad to worse when 15,000 war surplus WLs were offered for public sale. It would be two more years before motorcycle production regained its pre-war level.

There was only one thing that had not changed in the forced interlude of war – Harley-Davidson's winning ways. In 1947, among other successes, seven of the first ten Daytona finishers rode Harleys. Over the next two years, 36 of 47 AMA championship events went to the Milwaukee marque.

Harley-Davidson took up residence in a second factory on Capitol Drive, Wauwatosa, in 1947. By 1948, production was at an all-time high and, more important to America's highways, the replacement for the noble Knucklehead made its first public appearance that same year. The Panhead as it became known, was a development of the Knuckle rather than an all-new concept. As well as a revised (and much more oil-tight) lubrication

■ LEFT *Before the appearance of the HydraGlide's telescopic forks, the first Panheads ran with the old girder-fork chassis, as with this magnificently restored 1948 example.*

system, the Pan featured aluminium alloy cylinder heads in place of the Knuckle's iron and hydraulic "lifters" rather than solid push-rods. The Pan, so named because its chrome-plated rocker covers resembled inverted baking pans, was built in both 74cu in (1,200cc) and 61cu in (1,000cc) sizes; the latter was discontinued in 1953. The larger version retained the "traditional" bore and stroke dimensions of 3⁷⁄₁₆ x 4in (87 x 101mm).

The first all-new model powered by the Panhead engine was the HydraGlide of 1949, so-called because it was the first Harley to incorporate hydraulically-damped, telescopic front forks. It was also, of course, the first model granted one of the most evocative titles in motorcycling: "Glide". The Panhead engine would do much to get the species on its famous way, propelling not only the DuoGlide of 1958 but the first of the ElectraGlides as well.

Though no-one knew it at the time, this first Glide was to set the visual cues for the "Retro-Tech" Harleys which would appear four decades later. From its deeply-valanced mudguards and its chromed fork shrouds to its stylized rear end, the style of modern Softails owes much to the HydraGlide.

■ **INTO THE 1950S**

Harley-Davidson styles of the 1950s were in many ways a contradiction of those with which the company is now synonymous. True, 1950s imagery rates high in current Harley design but the decade began under the cloud of the Hollister "riots" of 1947, which tarnished the

■ RIGHT *Another perfectly restored example of a 1948 Panhead.*

■ LEFT *Even the hottest side-valve Model K, the KHK, was unable to run with European overhead valve (ohv) sports machines which stole Harley's thunder during the 1950s.*

Even if the typical Harley owner of the day could handle the tarnished image of the motorcycle he loved, he may have been less sanguine about another development: in 1947, the world's foremost manufacturer of big V-twins began the manufacture of two strokes.

image of motorcycling and alarmed motorcycle manufacturers. The true creator of the riots, however, was the media (including *Life* magazine) which represented the gathering in Hollister as a major assault on small-town America. The world was just getting over the shock when the Hollister-inspired film *The Wild One* was released in 1953, reopening old wounds. Although the film's star, Marlon Brando, rode a Triumph Thunderbird on screen, many people still swear it was a Harley.

■ RIGHT AND BELOW *The Model K-derived KRTT fared better on the track, whilst on the street, their slowness made them popular with the insurers of Hollywood stars.*

This seemingly radical departure was an attempt to bring Milwaukee's appeal to a wider market, a move that was applauded at the time by many observers.

The line began with the 125cc Model S, a 1.7 horsepower machine based on the same German DKW RT125 design as the BSA Bantam, the rights to which both companies acquired as part of Germany's war reparations. More than 10,000 were built in the model's debut year, based on the expensive misconception that war veterans would buy almost anything with wheels, before production slipped to a more realistic 4,000 or so per annum. The engine grew to 165cc in 1954, powering the Models ST and Super Ten before increasing to 175cc for the Ranger/Pacer/Scat series in 1962. Perhaps Harley's best-known lightweights were the 125cc Model B Hummer, produced from 1955–59, and the 165cc Topper Scooter of the early 1960s.

■ ABOVE *The HydraGlide was special, but something was missing...*

■ BELOW *...this came with the DuoGlide, the first Harley big twin to feature real suspension at both ends.*

Unfortunately, other manufacturers were also intent on broadening their markets. Harley-Davidson had by now introduced dealer demonstrator models and was to lose one competitor with the demise of Indian in 1953, but Triumph's creation of a vibrant new American import network in 1951 was a major alarm.

Isolated by war and supported by military production, Harley had enjoyed easy pickings for too long. Triumph – along with other British marques such as BSA, Norton and Royal Enfield – had a range of cheaper yet much more exciting and technically sophisticated models than Harley-Davidson (whose flagship model persisted with hand-gear-change until 1952).

Harley's response was heavy-handed and ultimately counter-productive as they attempted to bully dealers into having no business with the British pretenders.

Milwaukee also went so far as to apply for federal trade protection in 1952, alleging that the British machines were being subsidized and "dumped" on the American market. They asked for a 40 per cent import tax and quotas on the number of machines that Triumph (and parent company BSA) could import.

Thirty years later, Harley would get the protection that it had wanted, this time against the Japanese. The first time around, however, the Government's Tariff Commission found that Triumph had no case to answer. Worse still, they told Harley to quit its restrictive trading practices – a ruling that was to have devastating echoes for the company in the decades ahead.

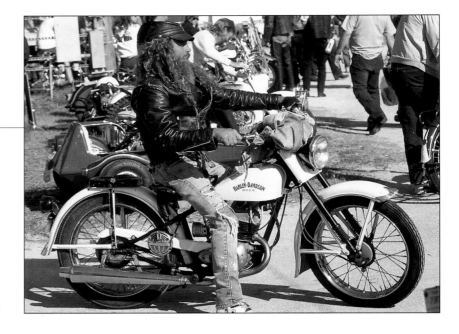

■ OLD, SLOW AND OBSOLETE

No model summed up Harley's problem more than the Model K, introduced in 1952 to replace the WL. The K was a heavy 45.3cu in (742cc) side-valve design compared to the overhead valves, lightweight construction and good suspension offered by British twins (and, in the case of Norton, arguably the finest handling motorcycle in the world). Granted, the K included proper suspension at both ends – a first for Milwaukee – but in virtually every other respect it was woefully outclassed by the British-made bikes.

Harley claimed 30 horsepower for the Model K, which was only a little less than the contemporary Triumph Thunderbird. Whether or not this was true, the 85mph (137kph) V-twin was no match for the 103mph (166 kph) British model, although the KK version, which had hotter cams, was better. Early Model Ks also had serious mechanical problems, although quality and power was improved by a capacity increase to 883cc for the 55-inch KH model in 1954.

■ ABOVE *Not quite King of the Road: a Milwaukee two-stroke.*

■ BELOW *The Shovelhead would replace the Panhead for the 1966 model year, as with this ElectraGlide.*

Remarkably, Paul Goldsmith took a K-based KR racer to victory by more than two miles (3km) in the Daytona 200 road race of 1953, a victory Harley-Davidsons were to repeat for the remainder of the decade. In 1954, the legendary Joe Leonard became first American national champion on KR and KR-TT racers. Although superficially impressive, these exploits owed much to the now familiar ploy of persuading the authorities to handicap the opposition. In this case, foreign ohv engines competing against 750cc Harley flatheads were limited to 500cc.

The K sold moderately well but overall sales figures show the full extent of Milwaukee's problem. In wheel-hungry 1948, Harley-Davidson produced more than 31,000 machines, the largest figure in its history. Yet by 1955, sales had plummeted to a low of less than 12,000. The problem could not be blamed on public disaffection with motorcycling, either – during the same period sales of imported machines went from strength to strength.

The machine which superseded the Model K in 1957 – the XL Sportster – was better in every way, eventually. The original Sportster's performance was lacklustre but by 1958 it benefited to the tune of 12 horsepower, due to lighter valve-gear, higher compression, larger ports and valves, and a legend was born.

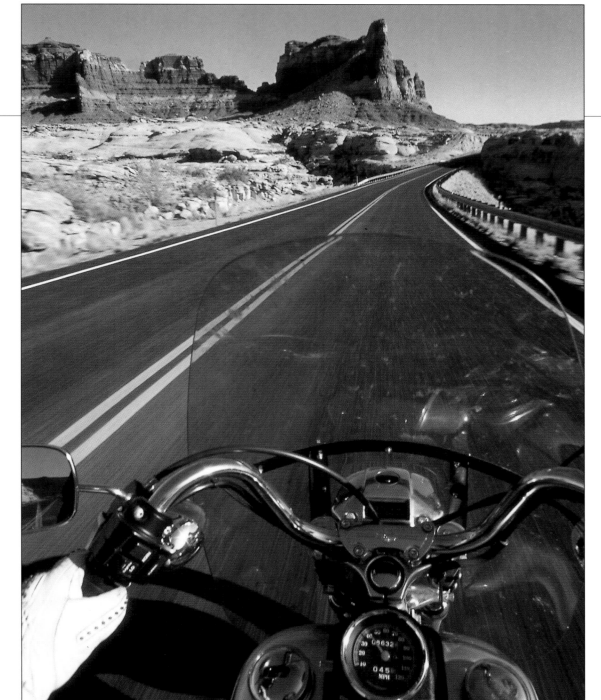

■ RIGHT *What Harleys are best at: cruising the vastness of the good ol' US of A.*

Displacing 53.9cu in (883cc), as today, the XL boasted unit construction for the engine and gearbox. Swing-arm rear suspension with car-type dampers allowed early Sportsters to be sold for either on- or off-road use. The XL was an instant hit, accounting for almost 20 per cent of Harley's 1957 production of more than 13,000 machines. In 1958, the stock XL was joined by one of the most legendary Harleys ever produced, the XLCH – "Competition Hot". Other variations have included the low-riding Hugger (1979) and the limited-edition XR1000 (1983). The Sportster is also father to the remarkable XR750 dirt oval racer.

■ RIGHT *The Topper scooter was another of Milwaukee's attempts to diversify. At best, these achieved very limited success.*

■ GLIDING INTO THE 1960S

As the 1950s drew to a close, the HydraGlide finally got the rear suspension it deserved and the Model F DuoGlide was born in 1958. The Duo featured a hydraulic rear brake as well as handsome two-tone styling and a swinging-fork rear end. However, this was something of an indulgence as both wheels contained puny six-inch drum brakes which struggled to slow down the Glide's substantial bulk, whatever their means of operation. The Duo is perhaps better remembered for film stardom – Dennis Hopper rode one in the cult movie *Easy Rider*.

With a new heavyweight on the block and the Sportster selling moderately well, Harley-Davidson renewed its attention to expanding its market base. One of the more successful measures was a move into glass-fibre moulding – initially boats, but later golf carts and motorcycle accessories. The main goal was still a foothold in the global boom in motorcycle sales. At the time, this meant lightweight machines, a demand to which the existing two-strokes were proving unequal. Sales of the ST

■ BELOW *Harley would surely have done better to concentrate on its core business, big V-twins, than on other models.*

were roughly similar to those of the Sportster, yet profit margins were much lower. Juneau Avenue's Development Committee, responsible for future planning, decided that collaboration with an overseas company might be the most effective way forward.

Consequently, Harley became half-owner of the motorcycle division of Aermacchi, or Aeronautica Macchi SpA, for just under $250,000. Harley anticipated the partnership would generate sales of 6,000 lightweight bikes per year, to be produced in Varese, Italy.

The first Harley-Aermacchi appeared in September 1960, quickly announcing its pedigree with a 1-2-3 result at the Santa Fe AMA short track championship races. The 250 Sprint was based on a spine-framed, horizontal, single-cylinder, four-stroke design similar to that of the famous Aermacchi racers, although most subsequent "joint venture" models would be small two-strokes. The 250 was light, powerful (the company claimed 21 horsepower, growing to 25 by 1964), handled well and spawned a line of superb racing machines.

Yet the Sprint and its fellow Macchis – and indeed Milwaukee's home-grown lightweights – all failed to live up to Harley's commercial expectations, for a variety of reasons. Communications between the company's headquarters in the United States and Varese were often poor, causing continuous supply problems with bought-in components and

incompatibility with American parts. Later, after the AMF take-over of Harley-Davidson in 1969, specifications were often changed erratically, without appropriate consultation or repricing. Most of all, the products were not wanted by a public being offered Japanese machines of ever-more sophisticated specification at lower prices (Honda had entered the American market in 1959). Nor were they wanted by dealers who had to carry new parts stock, retrain staff and relearn their business – all for a much smaller profit margin.

There were high-points, though – not least Walter Villa's consecutive world 250cc road-race titles in 1974 and 1975. The four-strokes got into the act: Roger Reiman took a Sprint-powered streamliner to a new world 250cc speed record of 156mph (251.05kph) in 1964, improved to 177mph (284.85kph) in 1965.

It was an unrewarding marriage and divorce came too late.

In June 1978, Harley closed its Italian factory. Juneau Avenue would never again aspire to a true mass market.

■ BELOW *ElectraGlide, possibly the most evocative badge in motorcycling.*

THE AMF YEARS

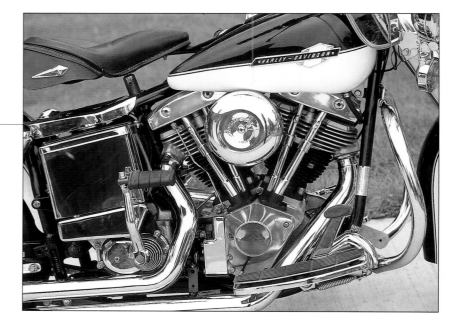

In 1964, Harley-Davidson not only unveiled its first new corporate logo in almost 60 years but also the model bearing possibly the most evocative name in the company's long history: ElectraGlide. Yet it was the following year that would be remembered as the more momentous. According to Harley lore, 1965 represented two climactic events. The first was the unveiling of a new generation of Shovelhead engines, replacing the venerable Panheads. Second, and ultimately more far-reaching, was the decision to list the company on the New York Stock Exchange – after more than 60 years as a family firm, its founding families were now to lose complete control.

More than 1.3 million Harley shares were sold in the four years that followed the original listing. They performed well and investors – and straightforward enthusiasts – felt good. Optimism was short-lived once again, however, as imported Japanese motorcycles made ever-increasing inroads in the American market. Initially, these machines were middleweights – light, fast, affordable and refined – but soon Honda would begin a full-frontal assault with the seminal four-cylinder CB750. The age of the high-performance "superbike" had arrived.

As Harley's fortunes ebbed and its shares dipped, it came under threat of takeover from an industrial conglomerate, Bangor Punta, which was busily accumulating Harley-Davidson stock. In 1968, fearful of the

■ ABOVE *Under AMF's ownership, sales improved but quality reputedly suffered, yet the Shovelhead soldiered on.*

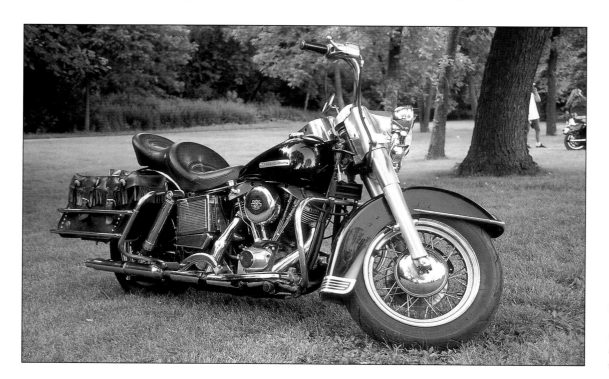

■ LEFT *80-inch (1,340cc) versions of the Shovelhead first appeared in 1978, as with this FLH.*

■ ABOVE LEFT *The ohv Sportster was a vast improvement on the sidevalve Model K.*

■ ABOVE RIGHT *More prized still was the tuned XLH Sportster, such as this example from 1972.*

sweeping changes proposed, company president William H. Davidson resumed talks with American Machine and Foundry (AMF).

AMF was another industrial giant with designs on Harley but with less of a predatory reputation (chairman Rodney C. Gott was a keen motorcyclist). Harley recommended AMF's offer to shareholders, most of whom did well out of the subsequent $21 million deal. So it was that on 18 December 1968, Harley-Davidson voted to merge with AMF, a move ratified by shareholders on 7 January 1969. Thus the American icon became AMF property, with Gott as chairman, although it wasn't until 1971 that the new owner's logo would be seen on Harley-Davidson machines.

Today, it is fashionable to believe that AMF starved and milked Milwaukee's finest, that it didn't understand motorcycles or motorcyclists, that quality went to the dogs and that Harley/AMF never built a decent bike. Some of this is probably true, but AMF did sink millions of dollars into its new project.c During its first three years in control, total sales more than doubled and, during its 12 years at the helm, sales of American-made machines more than tripled. In addition, the company diversified into such unlikely fields as snowmobiles and desert racers. Sales were reasonably strong but profits, unfortunately, were not.

Difficult labour relations at Capitol Drive were another concern. As a consequence of the

■ RIGHT *The look was still there, as with this flathead, but quality was declining as Harley struggled to keep pace with a changing market.*

tension, the bulk of production was moved to a vacant AMF plant in York, Pennsylvania (where it remains to this day, although Milwaukee has always made engines).

More exciting developments were afoot. 1970 brought a whole new kind of iron, the FX1200 SuperGlide. This was the first of a string of startling cosmetic innovations from the fertile mind of William G. Davidson. Just as crucial was AMF's marketing and promotion expertise, which certainly rubbed off on the future, independent Harley-Davidson company.

■ EXCITING IRON

If the 1970s was a commercially disastrous decade for Harley-Davidson, the hardware it produced at least paved the way for better times to come. Nowhere was this more evident than with the SuperGlide, the first major new twin launched by Harley after the takeover by

■ ABOVE *"AMF" on the tank was not well received by many, but others still considered the ElectraGlide the king of the road.*

■ LEFT *The King of the Road title actually referred to optional touring accessories. Bolt-on parts and other "goodies" would become huge business in later years.*

■ ABOVE *A 1972 ElectraGlide: no other motorcycle could get away with a white leather seat.*

AMF. The SuperGlide's hybrid philosophy – a little bit from one model, some from another and more parts from a third – became the essence of all the most memorable Harleys produced since. Despite the splash it made at the time – most road tests praised the Super-Glide expansively – early examples were

distinctly under-specified for the new "superbike" age. Disc brakes arrived in 1973 and an electric start option, the FXE, in 1974.

By 1977, Willie G. launched another classic derivative: the FXS Low Rider, complete with standard highway pegs, Fat Bob two-piece petrol tank and a seat just 27in (685mm) above the ground. Later the same year, the XLCR Café Racer was launched. This sinister all-black device was too radical a statement to enjoy much sales success at the time, but is a highly-prized collector's piece today.

The range of options increased further with the introduction of the 80-inch (1,340cc) Shovelhead engine, initially on the Electra-Glide in 1978. This led to the FLH one year later, offered as standard with a complete set of touring extras, later to become the long-haul norm: saddlebags, luggage rack, fairing, running boards and additional lights. This in turn led to the FLT TourGlide of 1980, similar to the full-dress Glide but with better brakes and a larger, twin headlamp touring fairing. More significantly, the FLT featured Harley-Davidsons' first five-speed transmission and, not least, its first use of rubber-mounting to protect the rider from engine vibration.

■ RIGHT *Twin filler caps, tank-top speedometer and lashings of chrome: all Harley hallmarks.*

■ OPPOSITE *Willie G. Davidson (second left) pictured at Daytona with the Japanese-built Sundance racer.*

In fact, 1980 can be viewed as a vintage year all round. The Super Glide cruiser became the FXB Sturgis, named after the famous rally held annually in South Dakota. The "B" represented the first toothed-rubber belt drive – a clean, smooth and trouble-free system now standard across the range. For good measure, there was the FXWG Wide Glide and FXEF Fat Bob.

■ ABOVE *Willie G. Davidson's immortal "factory custom": the trend-setting SuperGlide.*

■ CHALLENGE FROM JAPAN

Nostalgia tells us that the 1970s produced a stream of classic Harley-Davidson models but, hardware aside, it was all an illusion. Even after shedding its Italian operation, the unpalatable truth was that, at the start of the 1980s, few people gave AMF Harley-Davidson very much chance of survival.

Who was to blame? It is tempting to point the finger at AMF, but whatever the company's shortcomings as custodians of the Milwaukee legend, Harley's biggest problem lay in a quite different direction. After all, it was scarcely AMF's fault that this period coincided so precisely with the rise to global domination of the Japanese motorcycle industry.

It is also a myth that Japan hijacked the American motorcycle market, either from Harley-Davidson or from the Europeans. Even after the British invasion of the mid-1950s, sales of new motorcycles in the United States stood at a paltry 60,000 units per year. By 1973, annual sales had soared to more than

two million. This staggering increase was almost solely due to the inventiveness and enterprise of the Japanese, who produced reliable, fast and exciting machines far more advanced than any Harley, at a far lower price. Whatever "image" Harleys possessed was undersold, with few buyers prepared to pay the premium. The AMF years had seen turnover grow from $49 million to over $300 million but profits were going into reverse.

Milwaukee's response was to allege cut-price "dumping" of Japanese models, as with Triumph 20 years earlier. The American International Trade Commission agreed that dumping had taken place but that the effective subsidy was almost negligible. It concluded that the practice had not significantly harmed Milwaukee's sales and that the principal cause of Harley's difficulties was self-imposed: its model range was obsolete.

More than a decade earlier, William H. Davidson had remarked that AMF "thought Harley-Davidson could become another

■ BELOW *Another SuperGlide, this time fitted with optional pillion backrest.*

Honda. That's ridiculous... we were never meant to be a high production company."

AMF had to some extent attempted to compete head-on with Japan rather than concentrating on the more specialized market that Harley suited best. Production figures for 1982 offer some measure of the hopelessness of such a strategy: Honda built more than 3.5 million bikes in the year; Harley built less than 50 thousand.

The situation was desperate. Just six short years after 1973, Harley's share of the rapidly growing American big-bike market had plunged from almost 100 per cent to less than 40 per cent.

Production in the United States plummeted from 75,000 motorcycles in 1975 to 41,000 in 1981. Dire labour relations had brought a 101-day strike in 1974 over cost-of-living wage increases. Some in the company saw this coming, despite an artificial

■ BELOW *Another symphony in metal from Willie G., the XLCR Café Racer.*

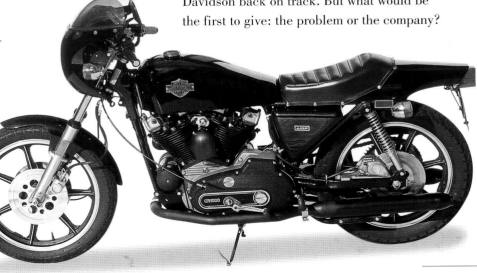

boost in 1978 due to the company's 75th birthday celebrations. Vaughn Beals, company president since 1977, and chief engineer Jeff Bleustein alerted top managers to the unpalatable realities. Beals set up a quality control and inspection programme that began to eliminate the worst of the problems, but all these measures were at a prodigious cost.

New initiatives slowly began to put Harley-Davidson back on track. But what would be the first to give: the problem or the company?

"THE EAGLE FLIES ALONE"

The year 1981 brought what was probably the most momentous – and certainly the most audacious – episode in the long history of Harley-Davidson. With AMF losing interest and patience, chairman Vaughn Beals persuaded 12 other Harley executives to join him in an $81.5 million leveraged buyout from AMF control. The group included Charlie Thompson, appointed president the previous year, and Willie G. Davidson. A letter of intent was signed on 26 February and the bid went public five days later at Daytona Beach. The group found a willing lead lender in Citicorp Bank and after several months of tough bargaining with AMF, the newly-independent Harley-Davidson Motor Co. began business on 16 June 1981. The event, not surprisingly, was accompanied by widespread rejoicing and fanfares, under the slogan "The Eagle Flies

Alone" – including a symbolic ride-out by the new owners, from Milwaukee to York, as well as a solid gold dipstick for the first bike built under the new regime. Harley-Davidson was

■ ABOVE *There's no mistaking the American roots of this early Evo FLH model.*

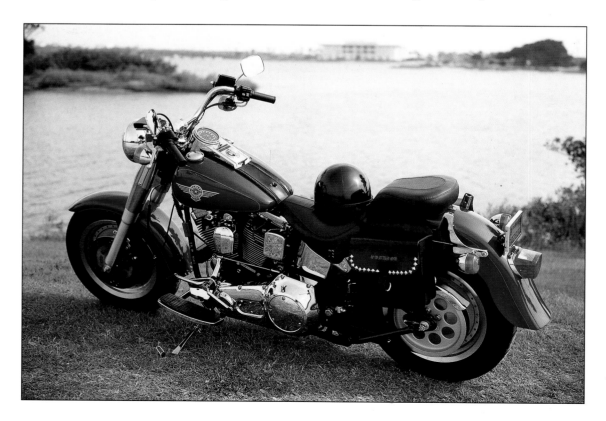

■ LEFT *One of the very first Evo engines in one of the very first Softail models, pictured here.*

ABOVE *As quality suffered, many US police forces spurned Milwaukee machines.*

finally owned and run by real motorcyclists, men who loved the big V-twins, men who really cared. They were heady days, but the euphoria counted for nothing on its own. The American market, and Harley-Davidson's part in particular, was about to cave in even further. The buy-out did not enhance the buyers' fortunes as much as had been hoped – the newly-independent company's share of the shrinking American big-bike cake had dropped to a mere 23 per cent by 1983.

Ownership may have changed but one fundamental truth had not: Harley-Davidson's competitors were still producing better bikes at lower cost.

Over-staffing was part of the problem, and almost 200 clerical jobs went almost at once, but there was much more to it. Put bluntly, Harley's – indeed, much of America's – manufacturing culture was antique. Beals and other managers had toured Japanese plants in 1980 but it wasn't until after the buyout, when they were given the opportunity to inspect the Honda assembly plant in Marysville, Ohio, that they began to understand fully.

BELOW LEFT *To confirmed Harley aficionados, nothing beat customizing, whether of an old Panhead...*

BELOW RIGHT *...or perhaps something more recent... a Shovelhead.*

As chairman Vaughn Beals remarked: "We found it hard to believe we could be that bad – but we were. We were being wiped out by the Japanese because they were better managers. It wasn't robotics, or culture, or morning callisthenics and company songs – it was professional managers who understood their business and paid attention to detail."

Beal's message wasn't lost on the new team. With help from industrial fixers Andersen Consulting, within four months pilot programmes for "just-in-time" statistical process control (Harley called this "MAN" – Materials As Needed) and other up-to-date production systems were initiated and staff levels were slashed from 3,800 to 2,200. Tom

Gelb, in charge of production, explained the situation to Harley-Davidson staff as directly as possible: "We have to play the game the way the Japanese play it or we're dead."

Quality and efficiency was one thing, getting the message across to potential customers quite another. The company shifted its marketing focus, stopped trying to compete against Japanese mainstream motorcycles and threw all of its resources into developing what we now take for granted as its uniquely American big-bike niche. (Along the way, a little-known project inherited from AMF for an overhead camshaft V-four was quietly dropped after several working prototypes were produced.) Was it too little, too late? Despite new models such as the five-speed FXR SuperGlide II and a new Sportster, the lone-flying eagle reported a loss of $25 million in 1982. It was going to be a close-run thing.

■ THE PRESIDENT STEPS IN

In August 1982, another Harley delegation made the trip to Washington, again alleging illegal trading practices by Japanese motorcycle companies. Yet again, the ITC was told that cheap motorcycles were being illegally dumped on the market and that the Japanese were "virtually copying" Harley models, all of which was seriously undermining their sales. This time Harley had a case, as

■ ABOVE LEFT *AMF did not realise how lucrative Harley lifestyle and hardware were to be in the future.*

■ ABOVE RIGHT *The Evolution engine, as in this 95th Anniversary 'Glide transformed Harley's fortunes.*

■ BELOW *Meanwhile, loading the heavyweights with goodies opened up a whole new field of Harley machines.*

massive over-supply in declining markets meant that many machines were sold at a loss. As Vaughn Beals put it, "We simply want the US government to restore order to a motorcycle market under siege by Japanese manufacturers who increased production in the face of sharp market decline."

As if to highlight the problem, the local Wisconsin police force bought Kawasaki motorcycles rather than Harleys, prompting a mass ride-out in protest from Capitol Drive.

The Commission duly found in Milwaukee's favour and recommended as much to President Ronald Reagan. On All Fools Day 1983, the White House confirmed that import tariffs were to be imposed on Japanese machines. The tariffs would apply to all imported models of

■ LEFT *The "CowGlide", Heritage Softail Nostalgia, coolest of all the Softails...*

■ ABOVE RIGHT *...although even this wasn't radical enough for some owners, as shown by this Springer Softail.*

more than 700cc, at the hefty rate of 45 per cent (in addition to the existing 4.4 per cent duty), decreasing year-by-year to 35, 20, 15 and 10 per cent until April 1988.

Although Japanese machines built in the United States, such as Honda Gold Wings, were exempt, the levy was inevitably a major asset to Harley-Davidson's regeneration. In the meantime, they had to continue to improve quality and efficiency. Perhaps most crucial of all, a credible replacement for the aged Shovelhead was long overdue. Short-term fixes such as the digital ignition introduced on the new FXRT in 1983 were no longer enough.

Harley threw $3 million into a "Super Ride" demonstration programme in 1984, to show that the company had solved its notorious quality-control problems. TV commercials invited bikers to visit any of its 600-plus dealers to road test a new Harley. Over three weekends, the company gave 90,000 rides to 40,000 people, half of whom owned other brands. At first, the venture didn't sell enough bikes to cover its cost, but it made the point.

Then there was HOG – the Harley Owners' Group. This was a major corporate effort to bring customers together in the Harley-Davidson lifestyle. Nothing so ambitious had ever been attempted by any motorcycle manufacturer, yet HOG proved uniquely suited to the Harley image. A runaway success, HOG now boasts almost half a million committed members worldwide and is a model for similar schemes by other motorcycle manufacturers.

The company also began to defend its name, copyrights and trademarks for the first time,

■ BELOW *Meanwhile, out on the open highway, Milwaukee's long-legged punch counts for more than mere paint.*

and vigorously. In future, if anyone wanted a Harley-Davidson logo, Milwaukee would demand its rightful royalties. Over half a century after pioneering the sale of branded accessories, Harley was at last determined to cash in on the image it had taken eight decades to create. Slowly, Vaughn Beals and his team began to turn the near-disaster around. Thanks to improvements in quality and efficiency, and more aggressive marketing, Harley began steadily to catch up with mighty Honda in the heavyweight division.

At last, this very American company was beginning to make the most of its uniquely American image. 1982's loss became a small surplus in 1983.

A year later, in 1984, Harley reported a profit of $2.9 million on sales of $294 million. Even though there was still a very long way to go, the eagle was on its way.

EVOLUTION

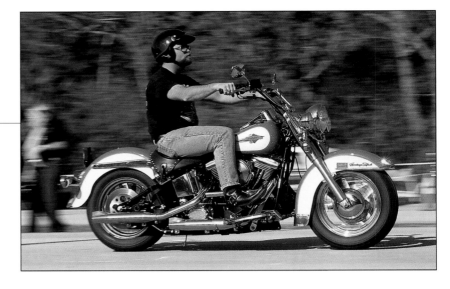

The anxiously-awaited replacement for the Shovelhead finally arrived in 1984 – and Harley-Davidson's future balanced precariously on a knife's edge. The V2 Evolution engine certainly looked like the answer to everyone's prayers. Despite a bottom-end with origins dating back to the 61E of 1936, it was an altogether better powerplant than the Shovelhead it replaced.

As the name suggests, the "Evo" is a development of the Shovel rather than a totally new design, yet almost every component was different and improved. Its cylinders, splayed at the "classic" 45 degrees, displace 81.8cu in or 1,340cc (although badges round this down to 80in). Scaling 20lbs (9kgs) less but producing 15 per cent more torque than its predecessor, the Evo would prove to be all it was cracked up to be.

In 1983, Harley-Davidson made sure its new baby created an impact with a publicity stunt to mark the company's 80th birthday celebrations: 8,000 miles (12,875

km) at an average of 80mph (128.7kph) with none of the routine servicing a customer's machine would receive on standard FLT Tour Glides. At Talladega Speedway in July 1983, the Evolution-engined TourGlides thundered through the designated 8,000 miles, but slightly off the scheduled pace: allowing for mishaps that never occurred, they averaged 85mph (136.8kph).

A brand-new engine was cause enough for celebration (helped perhaps by the new H-D brand beer), but the first model powered by the Evo engine was a landmark in its own right. This was the 1984 FXST Softail, and with it came a whole new concept in motorcycle style and design. With its fake "hardtail" rear end, gleaming chrome and low, rounded lines, the Softail was a

■ ABOVE *Cruisin' through town can just look so cool.*

■ BELOW *Retro-Tech: the hardtail look of this Heritage Softail is clear. The system uses twin shock absorbers hidden beneath the engine.*

■ ABOVE *"Basic" Softails retain telescopic front forks.*

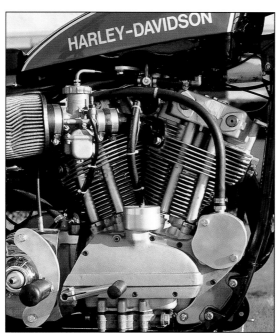

■ RIGHT *At the opposite extreme is this road-registered XR750 racer, as used in US dirt-track competition.*

strident echo of motorcycles of the 1950s: the age of Retro-Tech had dawned. Sportsters still cut a dash, especially with the launching of the new XR750-inspired XR1000. A year later, the Heritage Softail followed the basic FXST.

Almost overnight – or so it seemed – Harley-Davidson had a credible range and, after the gremlins of the Shovelhead years, a reputation for the dependability that had once been its hallmark. Again it had a product capable of meeting the demands of the California Highway Patrol (CHiPs) who, after a decade mounted on Kawasakis and Moto Guzzis, in 1984 ordered 155 FXRP Police Specials.

To Harley insiders, however, the "Evo year" was probably far more memorable for the financial strife which continued to undermine them. In 1984, Citicorp Bank, underwriter of the original buy-out, was becoming concerned that Harley's future might not be so rosy once the tariff on foreign competitors ended in 1988. Reasoning that the best time to get a good price for the company was when sales were still on the rise, they moved quickly, hitting Harley's directors with the bombshell: all credit facilities would be severely restricted from the following year.

This was a major blow to Harley's ambitious plans and the survival of the entire buy-out. Harley-Davidson was broke.

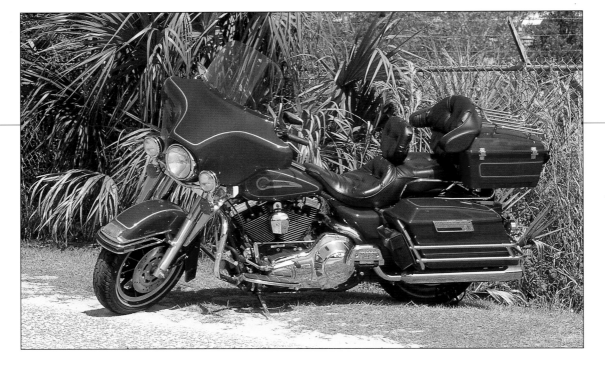

■ LEFT *ElectraGlides and TourGlides evolved ever-more luxury features such as cruise control, CB radio and intercoms.*

■ TURNING BACK THE TIDE

"Hawking begging bowls around Wall Street" was how Vaughn Beals described his desperate response. Over the summer of 1985, Beals and chief financial officer Richard Teerlink (later to succeed Beals as H-D's head), chased in vain after new lenders. Then, with the situation looking hopeless and lawyers drafting bankruptcy plans, Dean Witter Reynolds put Beals and Teerlink in touch with the Heller Financial Corporation. Luckily for Beals, Heller's second-in-command, Bob Koe, was a long-time Harley buff and willing to listen. He was impressed by what he heard, and on 23 December 1985 a financial package was agreed – the best Christmas present for which Harley could have wished.

The rescue package turned out to be a good deal for everyone but Citicorp, who had badly underestimated the outlook for this vibrant new Harley-D. Including credits, the bank received $49 million for the deal, $2 million less than it had poured in. Harley received $49.5 million of working capital. In a supreme irony, Harley recovered the Number One spot from Honda a year after being abandoned by Citicorp, with 33 per cent of the over-850cc American market. The long struggle to improve production

■ LEFT *Detail of the striking Ultra Classic ElectraGlide.*

■ BELOW *In stark contrast was the Sportster series, of which this 1984 XR-1000 is surely the best looking and most prized.*

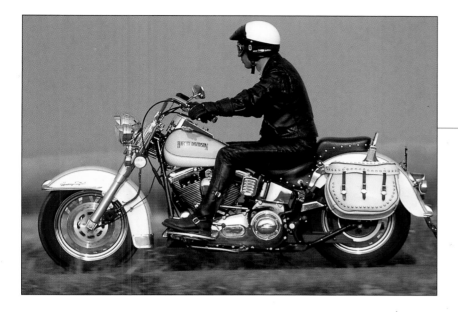

■ ABOVE *In Europe, as well as the United States, Evo Harley sales began to boom. This Heritage Softail Classic thunders across the Belgian Ardennes.*

and marketing, and regenerate the model range was beginning to pay dividends. 1986 profits were $4.3 million on sales of $295 million.

Harley's financial base was secured in June 1987 by floating the company on the New York Stock Exchange. The offer raised more than £30 million, allowing the company to reschedule its debts and buy the Holiday Rambler Corporation, a leading manufacturer of recreational vehicles. In October, the manufacturing rights to the military MT500 motorcycle were acquired from the British

Armstrong company. Less comforting was the closure of the competition department, though it made sound financial sense. Production of XR750 dirt-track engines was unaffected, and racing continued in the famous livery through independent dealer teams.

The most impressive news of all came on 17 March. In what turned out to be a public-relations triumph, Harley had taken the unprecedented step of asking that trade protection be removed a year ahead of schedule. As Vaughn Beals explained at the time, Harley-Davidson "no longer need tariff relief to compete with the Japanese". The chairman highlighted "the strong message… to the international community: US workers… can become competitive in world markets." Harley was again "the pride of America".

This was brought home best of all by President Ronald Reagan. After touring the York factory in Pennsylvania in May 1987, he

■ RIGHT *In places such as Florida's Daytona Beach, Harleys inspire crowds of fans of American iron. Fittingly, this is the famous Iron Horse Saloon.*

hailed the turnaround in Harley-Davidson's fortunes as "an American success story". And how right he was.

A major contribution to future success was tied up with the XLH 883 Sportster. With a price tag of just under $4,000 when introduced, the 883 was the type of entry-level machine so conspicuously absent from the Milwaukee stable in the past. In 1987, 883 owners got an even better deal with the announcement of Harley's innovative buy-back scheme: "Trade in your XLH against an FX or FL within two years and we'll guarantee $3,995 on your old machine."

Major new models included the stunning Heritage Softail Classic, ElectraGlide Sport and Low Rider Custom. By the end of 1987, Harley had 47 per cent of the American "super-heavyweight" market, a figure which would rise to 54 per cent just one year later. At last, Harley-Davidson was on its way.

■ SPRINGING AHEAD

1988 saw the debut of the largest-capacity Sportster ever – the 1100 grew to the full 1200cc of the XLH 1200. 1988 also brought a revamped FXRS Low Rider with improved forks and twin-cap Fat Bob fuel tank. Most striking of all was the model chosen to mark

H-D's 85th birthday, the FXTS Springer Softail. The Springer was a radical step both forward and back. Looking like a 1950 classic, it dispensed with the telescopic front end in favour of gleaming, chromed, lookalike girders. For the first time, a Harley had Retro-Tech at both ends and, almost overnight, became the style king of the Milwaukee range.

Within a year, the Springer and new Low Rider were joined by "Ultra Classic" versions of the all-conquering TourGlide and Electra-Glide models. These luxurious machines came equipped with a host of extras as standard, including cruise control, cigar lighter, intercom, CB radio and a sophisticated stereo hi-fi system. These were, and remain, the best-equipped and most expensive models in the Harley-Davidson range.

Ironically, as standard equipment became even more comprehensive, there was counter demand for a model more like the stripped-down Glides of the 1970s, such as the handsome FLHS ElectraGlide Sport introduced two years earlier. The FLHR Road King of today is in much the same mould as its handsome predecessor.

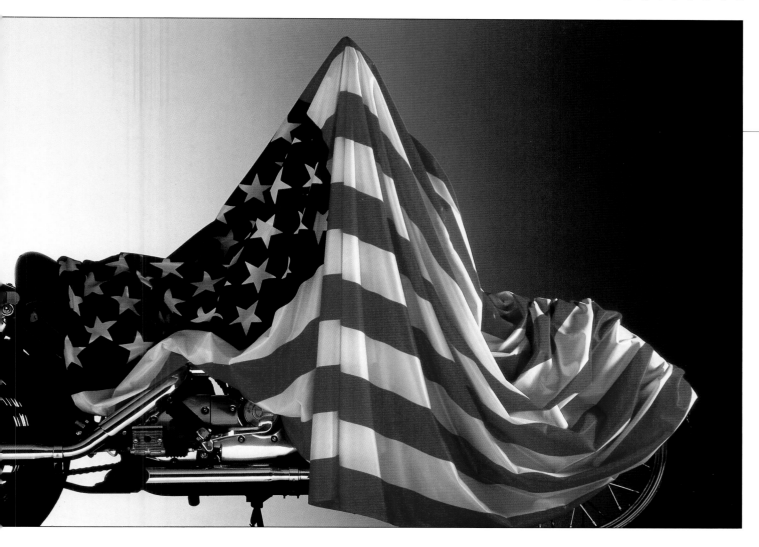

In 1989, a revamped clothing division – "MotorClothes" – was launched. MotorClothes, allied with Harley-Davidson's flourishing aftermarket hardware accessories, accounts for a substantial portion of overall annual profits. It is now possible to buy anything from bowie knives to toiletries bearing the celebrated H-D motif. Since the early 1990s there have been "Harley" shops that sell no motorcycles at all. The company's image had been transformed from a sick joke to the height of fashion.

With this priceless image came a turnaround in overall fortunes, from near-broke leviathan to glorious sales success. The foundations were varied: much-improved manufacturing of a broader, better model range allied to shrewd financial management, as well as inspired marketing. Production methods had witnessed a revolution, with each worker both a vital part

■ BELOW *During the 1990s' DynaGlides evolved from Low Riders to become one of the core elements of the Milwaukee line-up.*

of the quality-control process and a partner in Harley-Davidson's affairs. The Evolution engine earned a deserved reputation for rugged durability, oil-tightness and general user-friendliness.

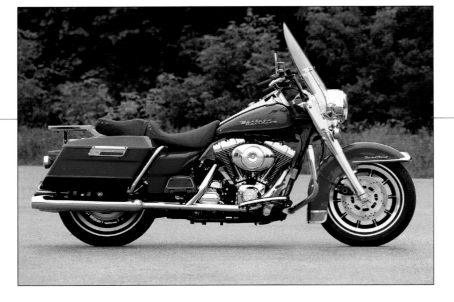

Not least was Harley-Davidson's good fortune in being located in the world's largest market for big-inch touring machines.

■ INTO THE 1990S

By the early 1990s, the tide had well and truly turned – indeed the boot was on the other foot. Annual production had reached more than 62,000 units, with 20 models accounting for 61 per cent of the American heavyweight market and more than 30 per cent of output exported to Milwaukee fans worldwide, double the figure of four years earlier. At the same time, sales of Japanese motorcycles were in steep decline, their dealers cutting margins or going out of business altogether.

New hardware continued to stream out of York. Many Harley fans rate the star of the 1990 catalogue as one of the most beautiful Harley-Davidsons ever created. "Fat Boy" was its unprepossessing title, yet the original FLSTF was an understated symphony in silver-grey. Later versions, in less restrained colours, never quite had the same class. The FXDB DynaGlide Sturgis, a mean and moody all-black cruiser unveiled for 1991, was the first of a new generation, and classy to boot.

If Milwaukee had any problems during the 1990s, one was encroaching noise and emissions regulations; the other the sheer difficulty of meeting soaring demand as

■ ABOVE *The moody Road King was a stylish attempt to return to the leaner, cleaner lines of the earliest ElectraGlides.*

■ BELOW *By the mid-1990s, top of the range Glides had added fuel injection to their extensive repertoire of "goodies".*

customers waited up to a year for their new dream machines. A major victory for environmental concerns was the first fuel-injected Harley roadster, the FLHTC-I Ultra Classic ElectraGlide, in 1985. Injection made the twin smoother, cleaner and more powerful than any previous Harley-Davidson.

Then came the Twin Cam 88 powerplant for 1999, which promised to take the same qualities even further. After four years and more than 2.5 million test miles (4 million km) under development, Harley-Davidson's new Twin Cam offers new levels of performance, reliability and durability.

Solving the supply problem involved a whirlwind programme of capital investment, culminating in the opening in 1998 of an $85 million Sportster plant at Kansas City. The spending began with the opening of a huge new automated paint plant at York in 1992. This $23 million facility finally broke York's crippling production bottleneck, taking manufacturing capacity beyond 110,000 machines per year.

■ RIGHT *For 1999, 15 years after the arrival of the redoubtable Evo, a new generation of Twin Cam 88 big twins hit the Harley scene.*

Accompanying this has been a hard-nosed commercial edge which began with the defence of trademarks – even including attempts to copyright the "Harley sound". To many die-hard fans, Harley's corporate clout sits uneasily alongside the image of easy-going, down-home virtues the company is at pains to present. Some might even prefer the mom-and-pop-corner-shop image of decades before – the one that almost went bust.

New Harleys might be objects of desire, but they are conceived and developed in an environment as implacably space-age as the bikes themselves are defiantly old-fashioned. The Willie G. Davidson Product Development Center was completed in 1997, at a cost of $40 million. Standing just a stone's throw from the existing Capitol Drive engine factory, it boasts a floor area of 213,000sq ft (20,000sq metres) under a graceful arc of concrete and glass, a structure befitting 21st-century ambitions. A new Big Twin powerline plant was also opened in 1997, located at nearby Menomonee Falls. Buell, now half-owned by Harley, assembles motorcycles in nearby East Troy, Wisconsin.

Harley-Davidson hasn't witnessed expansion like this since the years either side of the First World War. In fact, 1998 marked the thirteenth consecutive year in which Harley-Davidson had achieved record earnings. Sales topped $2,000 million for the first time, with output totalling 150,818 machines.

Thanks largely to the impetus provided by Kansas, production capacity is planned to reach 200,000 units.

For Harley-Davidson, the future of motorcycling at Milwaukee is looking good.

■ BELOW *The Deuce, introduced for the year 2000, sports the latest balance-shafted Twin Cam 88B engine.*

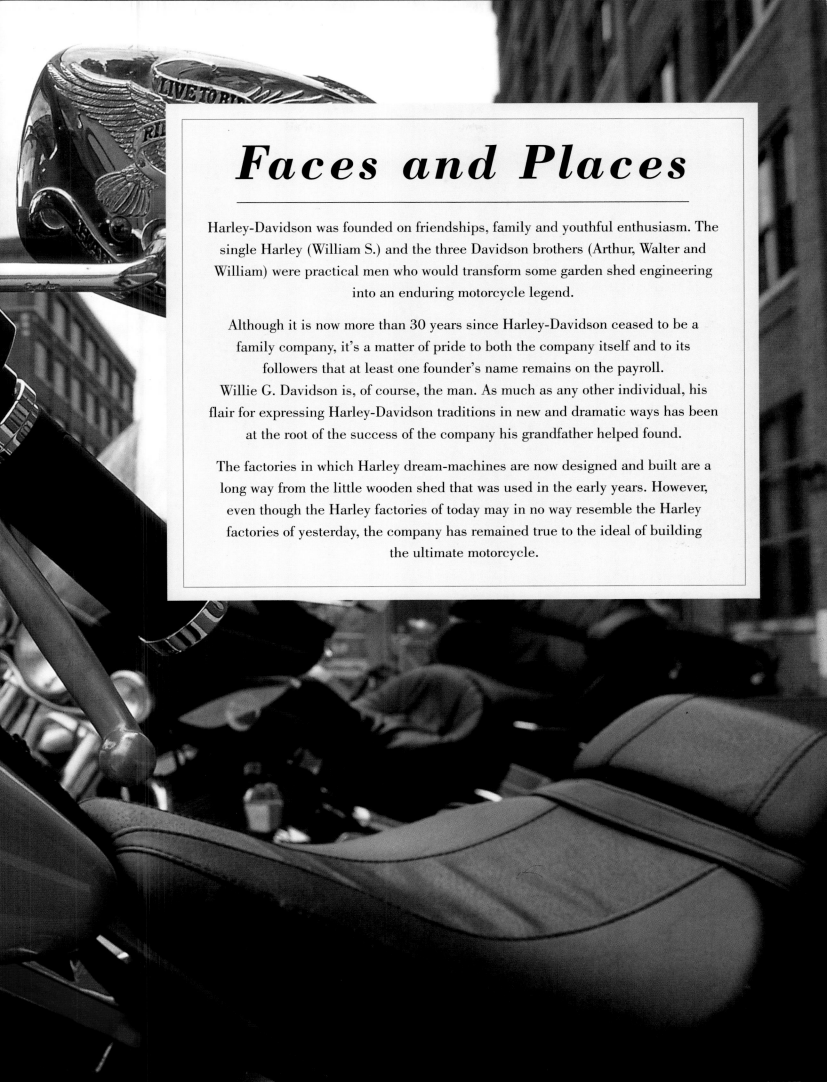

Faces and Places

Harley-Davidson was founded on friendships, family and youthful enthusiasm. The single Harley (William S.) and the three Davidson brothers (Arthur, Walter and William) were practical men who would transform some garden shed engineering into an enduring motorcycle legend.

Although it is now more than 30 years since Harley-Davidson ceased to be a family company, it's a matter of pride to both the company itself and to its followers that at least one founder's name remains on the payroll.
Willie G. Davidson is, of course, the man. As much as any other individual, his flair for expressing Harley-Davidson traditions in new and dramatic ways has been at the root of the success of the company his grandfather helped found.

The factories in which Harley dream-machines are now designed and built are a long way from the little wooden shed that was used in the early years. However, even though the Harley factories of today may in no way resemble the Harley factories of yesterday, the company has remained true to the ideal of building the ultimate motorcycle.

THE FOUNDERS

■ WILLIAM S. HARLEY

"Young Bill" began work at the age of 15 in a Milwaukee bicycle factory, and even as an enthusiastic dabbler soon showed engineering skills. As able in the saddle as he was in the workshop, he later became Harley-Davidson's chief engineer and treasurer, positions he held until his death from heart failure on 18 September 1943.

On graduating from university in 1908, he had set about designing Harley's first successful V-twin, which appeared the following year, although it was 1911 before the design became as dependable as earlier singles.

Bill was later responsible for a host of classic Harleys, not to mention the first clutch, kick start and many other developments. In 1914, he established the factory's race shop, which scored 26 major wins in its first season. During both world wars, his contacts with the military were vital to the company's (and the nation's) success. Active in the governing body of American bike racing, the American Motorcycle Association (AMA), he was also a keen wildlife photographer in private life.

■ ARTHUR DAVIDSON

A pattern-maker by trade, Arthur had the reputation of being the most outgoing of the founders, his energetic temperament making him particularly suited to sales. Arthur became the company's secretary and general sales manager, roles he discharged with distinction until his death in a car accident on 30 December 1950, at the age of 69. His own son, James, and James' wife, were also to die in a road accident 16 years later.

Perhaps Arthur's most lasting legacy was the establishment of Harley-Davidson's nationwide and international dealer networks. Beginning

in 1910, he had no fewer than 200 American outlets by 1912, later expanding to include official Harley-Davidson dealerships as far away as Australia and New Zealand. In the early years he practically ran the AMA "because there was no-one else around". After the Second World War, he spent an increasing amount of time at his farm in Waukesha County where he raised prize-winning Guernsey cattle.

■ WALTER S. DAVIDSON

Trained as a mechanic and machinist, Walter was a naturally gifted rider who brought the emergent Harley-Davidson company its first competition success. In June 1908, he entered a Harley-Davidson single in a two-day endurance run in New York's Catskill Mountains. The sole Harley in a field of 61, he scored a "perfect" 1,000 points, outstripping all of the preferred bikes. One month later, Walter was at it again, winning a Long Island economy run at no less than 188mpg (66km/litre) over 50 miles (80.5 kilometres).

Walter is best remembered, however, as Harley-Davidson's first president. Generous and scrupulously honest, he also became a

■ ABOVE *The founders, left to right: William A. Davidson, Walter Davidson, Arthur Davidson and William S. Harley.*

■ RIGHT *Harley-Davidson's first "factory", a 15 x 10ft wooden shed.*

director of First Wisconsin, the state's biggest bank. Walter died on 7 February 1942, still in charge at Juneau Avenue.

■ WILLIAM A. DAVIDSON

If Walter was the head of the company, "Old Bill" Davidson was regarded as its heart and driving force. Perhaps the least able rider of the foursome, Bill quickly found his niche as works manager, a vital position in a company expanding as quickly as Harley-Davidson. A big, burly character equally at home hunting and fishing as on the factory floor, he had a generous but paternalistic attitude to Harley's employees. Despite his bitter opposition, the factory first became unionized in April 1937. Within two years, Old Bill was gone, the victim of diabetic complications and the first of the founders to die. His son, William H., believed the stress of losing the battle to the unions hastened his father's death.

■ SECOND GENERATION

In the late 1920s, the founders' sons began to join the company. William H. Davidson joined in 1928, although he had worked on the shop floor while a student at the University of Wisconsin. A year later, he was joined by Gordon and Walter C. (both sons of Walter S.)

■ RIGHT *The famous Juneau Avenue factory, which was a large step up from the wooden shed.*

Davidson, William J. Harley and, later, John E. Harley. Of the other sons, Allan Davidson, son of William A., worked only briefly for the company and died young; Arthur Davidson Jr. made a successful business career in his own right. Four of these "first generation founders" were to make major contributions to the American icon the company would become.

William J. Harley succeeded his father as the company's chief engineer. He became vice president in charge of engineering in 1957, a position he held until his death in 1971. A connoisseur of fine wines and cheeses, he evidently needed little encouragement to visit the Harley-Davidson factory in Varese, Italy, after the take-over of Aermacchi.

John E. Harley, younger brother to William J., was elected to the board in 1949 and ran the Harley parts and accessories business, today one of Milwaukee's major profit centres. He rose to the rank of major during the Second World War, including a spell instructing army motorcyclists.

Walter C. Davidson ultimately followed his uncle Arthur as vice president of sales, earning a reputation during the Second World War as the man who could somehow get materials other companies could not. After the war, he fought Harley's increasingly rebellious dealer network, as Triumph and BSA in particular began offering cheaper and faster products in the American market. Harley's efforts to hold

■ ABOVE *The Founders inspect the first Knucklehead to roll off the Juneau Avenue production line for the 1936 model year.*

■ RIGHT *During the Second World War John E. Harley, younger brother of William J., was responsible for training army motorcyclists on bikes such as the one pictured.*

the fort not only backfired at the time but were to lead to legislation which would later open the door for the Japanese. When AMF took over the company in 1968, Walter saw the writing on the wall and took early retirement.

William H. Davidson, the son of William A., made the most lasting mark of all. A skilled rider (he won the prestigious Jack Pine Enduro in 1930 riding a Model 30DLD), he was later described as "the mortar that cemented the company". He joined Harley-Davidson full-time in 1928, was elected to the board in 1931 and became vice president six years later. For the next five years, he was the driving force behind Harley-Davidson's vital government contract work. When Walter S. died, William H. was the obvious candidate to lead the company, becoming president "by common consent" 16 days later, on 23 February 1942.

William H. had no doubts about where the company's future lay: "We tried for a long time to convince people that motorcycles had some

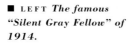

■ LEFT *The famous "Silent Gray Fellow" of 1914.*

■ RIGHT *The 2000 Harley model: the Deuce.*

utility value," he once presciently observed, "[but they] have never been anything but pleasure." In 1971, three years after the AMF takeover, he was appointed chairman of Harley-Davidson, but felt that the new company had "pulled my teeth" and soon resigned. Nor did he fully share AMF's ambitions, observing with typical foresight that AMF "thought Harley-Davidson could become another Honda. That's ridiculous... we were never meant to be a high production company."

■ **WILLIE G. DAVIDSON**

Willie G. is a remarkable man from a family of remarkable men. Yet it's perhaps surprising that he began his working life not with Harley-Davidson, but cutting his teeth with Ford and Excalibur cars. By the time he joined his grandpa's company in 1963, he had a broad schooling in industrial design – although he had also found time to design a new Harley-Davidson tank logo in 1957. He has spent most of the intervening years as vice president of styling – arguably the single most important role in such an image-conscious company. In another quirk of fate in which Harley seems to specialize, the model that made Willie G.'s name, the FX Super Glide of 1971, was the first major new model produced by the much-maligned AMF. A decade later, he was one of the prime movers of the buy-out from AMF orchestrated by chairman Vaughn Beals.

AMF's hold on Harley-Davidson may not have lasted but Willie G.'s has. During the week, his domain is the Willie G. Davidson Product Development Center, a space-age structure of steel and glass tucked behind the Sportster Engine Plant on Wauwatosa's Capitol Drive. Yet to the biking world he's the man in the trade-mark black beret at gatherings such as Sturgis and Daytona Bike Week, ogling hardware just like any other Harley fan.

Willie G. has an uncommonly successful stylist's touch, yet he also has the common touch. To many he *is* Harley Davidson, and when he finally hangs up his leathers, there are two Davidsons waiting in the wings. Son Bill, who joined the firm in 1984, runs HOG, while daughter Karen runs the MotorClothes division. Harley-Davidson is truly a family affair.

■ BELOW *Willie G. Davidson, grandson of the founder, and a great guiding spirit of Harley.*

HARLEY-DAVIDSON FACTORIES

William S. Harley and the Davidson brothers first went into production in 1904 in a shed hastily thrown up in the Davidson backyard, bearing the grand legend "Harley Davidson Motor Co." on its humble wooden door. These days, the location of the famous shed, 38th and Highland Boulevard, is owned by a company producing something else for which Milwaukee is famous – the huge Miller Brewing Company.

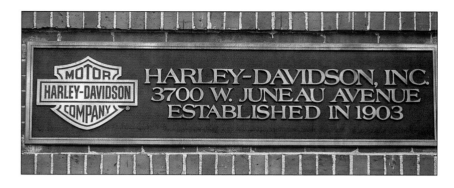

■ JUNEAU AVENUE

The founders took on their first employee in 1905, and moved into their first building on the present Juneau Avenue site twelve months later (although the road was then called Chestnut Street). In that year another five workers joined the Harley bandwagon as production soared to 50 motorcycles. Progress was relentless – and punishing. Walter Davidson later described how "we worked

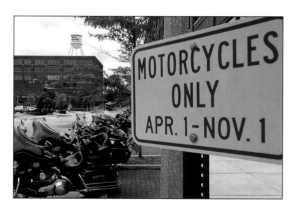

■ ABOVE *3700 Juneau Avenue, possibly the most famous address in motorcycling.*

■ LEFT *Like it says, "motorcycles only".*

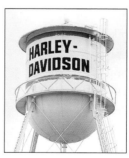

■ ABOVE *On Juneau Avenue, even the water is branded Harley-Davidson.*

■ LEFT *Now more than 80 years old, the former main factory is a protected historical site.*

■ LEFT AND BELOW *The Juneau Avenue factory now houses only management and administrative personnel, but echoes to almost a century of Harley's history.*

every day Sunday included, until at least 10:00. I remember it was an event when we quit work on Christmas night at 8:00 to attend a family reunion."

So it continued: 1907 – around 150 machines built, including the first police Harleys; 1908 – 18 employees and production tripled again to 450 units. By this time, manufacturing was in Harley-Davidson's first brick building, with a floor area of 2,380sq ft (220sq metres).

Such was the pressure to grow and get new bikes through the door that workers recall "putting machinery in place and starting production before the cement was dry". From 1907 to 1914, the Harley facility at least doubled in size every single year. At the outbreak of war in Europe, 1,574 employees built more than 16,000 machines in a factory of almost 300,000sq ft (28,000sq metres). With no exaggeration, the Milwaukee Journal described the company's breakneck progress as a "modern miracle".

Wartime pressure for space became so intense that the company once threw up a 2,400sq ft (220sq metre) brick building, only to tear it down and build something even bigger six months later. Buildings were leased on a temporary basis all over Milwaukee. Even Prohibition came to the company's aid, in a

■ BELOW *The Harley "bar and shield" is as recognizable in Morocco as here in Milwaukee.*

manner far more benign than Al Capone's. When breweries became idle, Harley-Davidson stepped in to rent the Pabst Brewing Company as storage space for Harley parts.

The post-war boom helped Harley-Davidson become, briefly at least, the largest motorcycle manufacturer in the world, pumping machines out of its huge, six-storey plant on Juneau Avenue, offering more than half a million square feet (50,000sq metres) of floor space on its completion in April 1919. The distinction

■ **LEFT AND RIGHT**
High-tech computerized machining is now part of the Harley way (left), but testing (right) is still hands-on. And could this man work for anyone else?

been no manufacturing at Harley's most evocative address: 3700 West Juneau Avenue, Milwaukee. Instead, the old site – and the grand old building – houses H-D's corporate headquarters and training departments.

■ **CAPITOL DRIVE**

No sooner had Harley sales begun to recover from the Depression of the 1930s (sales slid to a pitiful 3,703 bikes in 1933) than Pearl Harbor was bombed and the United States entered the war. Towards the end of the 1940s, the company was looking to expand again as markets recovered. At the end of 1948, Harley moved into its first new address for 42 years, in the Milwaukee suburb of Wauwatosa.

lasted only until the Depression of 1920, when annual sales collapsed from more than 28,000 to just 10,202. America's economy recovered from this slump but motorcycle sales somehow did not. It was 1942 before Harley sales again exceeded 1920 levels. Under these circumstances, the last thing Milwaukee needed was more plant. Since its conversion to offices and warehousing in 1973, there has

■ **BELOW LEFT**
Sportster engines awaiting shipment from Capitol Drive to Kansas.

■ **BELOW RIGHT**
Heavyweight engines are now made at Pilgrim Road before shipment to York for their final assembly.

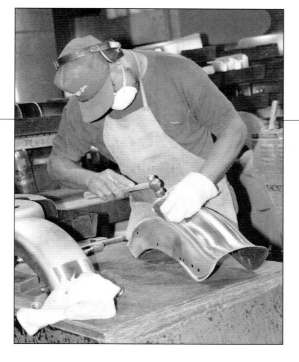

■ RIGHT *For finishing items such as mudguards, no machine can match a craftsman, as here at the factory in York, Pennsylvania.*

Thus, Capitol Drive, a single-story building of more than 260,000sq ft (24,000sq metres) which had previously housed the A. O. Smith propeller plant, became Harley-Davidson's second manufacturing centre. In anticipation of a boom in post-war demand for motorcycles (and the opposite for aircraft propellers), the factory had been bought for $1.5 million two years earlier. Harley dealers – introduced to

the new facility in a night-time "mystery tour" – weren't the only ones impressed.

Within a year, production was at an all-time high, although tougher times lay ahead. Also, less auspiciously (for V-twin die-hards, at least), November 1947 marked the debut of the 1.7 horsepower Model S 125cc single – a two-stroke Harley, heaven forbid. This was based on the same German DKW RT125 design as the BSA Bantam (and later Yamaha's very first model, the YA1 "Red Dragonfly") – and not least on the expectation that demobbed GI's would buy almost anything with wheels.

It was to be decades before the potential of Capitol Drive was fully realized, however. From today's viewpoint, it's difficult to envisage the trials cash-starved Harley-Davidson faced after that first burst of post-war optimism. During the 1950s, Harley sales were totally outstripped by British imports. From 31,000 units in 1948, sales never exceeded 17,250

■ RIGHT *Capitol Drive, home of Sportster engines and the official Harley Visitor Center.*

■ ABOVE *"Heavy powertrains" – Evo engines – awaiting shipment to York.*

again until 1965 – and for most of that time they were nearer 12,000. Paradoxically, matters only began to improve when the mass arrival of Japanese motorcycles stimulated wider interest in two-wheelers. Sales averaged around 30,000 for the remainder of the 1960s, rising to 70,000 by the mid-1970s.

This latter upturn in sales was due largely to AMF's heavy investment in manufacturing space, much of which is still in use today. The biggest single purchase was a $4.5 million monster for machining five-speed cases. Prior to this, Juneau Avenue had been a model of inefficiency, with part-assembled machines wheeled about and moved from shop to shop in lifts. Engine assembly moved from Juneau Avenue to Capitol Drive in 1971, although Harley-Davidson headquarters continued to undertake engine painting and the assembly of XR race engines for some years, the last actual manufacturing at the original site.

The addition of a modern facade means the Capitol Drive site no longer looks like a war-time propeller plant, but behind the facade the old factory now makes "small powertrains" for final assembly at Buell and the new Sportster plant in Kansas City. The facility also houses Harley's official Visitor Center, as well as a new customer engine reconditioning plant which is quite unique among volume motorcycle manufacturers.

■ RIGHT *Chrome and glass: a Springer guards The Willie G. Davidson Product Development Center (PDC), where the dreams of the future are generated.*

■ RIGHT *The PDC is
located to the rear of
the "small powertrains"
plant on Capitol Drive.*

■ BELOW *Many Harley
employees favour
motorcycles, but winter
in Milwaukee is no
place to be riding them.*

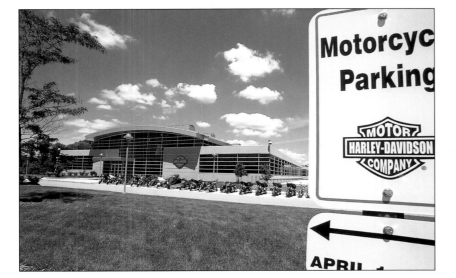

■ **VARESE**

With the exception of the original wooden sheds, Harley-Davidson has never abandoned one of its permanent sites on American soil. Overseas, however, it is a different story.

Milwaukee's Italian connection arose out of a desire to diversify into smaller, cheaper models, in order to hoist itself out of the financial mire of the 1950s. In 1960, Harley bought half of Aermacchi's two-wheeler division, based in Varese, Italy. The purchase was seen as a more sensible means of expanding the Harley-Davidson range than actually trying to develop new, cheaper models from scratch. In September 1960, the first Italian Harley emerged. This was the 250cc four-stroke Sprint, although two-strokes later predominated. (Although a stinkwheel Harley may sound like an offence against nature, lightweight two-strokes were produced in Milwaukee from 1947 until 1965.)

The joint venture didn't quite work out as hoped, but it did give Milwaukee its first and only world road race titles, with Walter Villa taking three 250cc and one 350cc crowns between 1974 and 1976, all on two-stroke twins. Roadster production was dogged by such absurdities as fitting American-made cables and controls to bikes built in Italy (where they made such things quite well).

Fundamentally, however, Varese couldn't compete with Japan. In June 1978, John A Davidson announced the closure of the project. The factory was bought by Cagiva which was producing 40,000 machines per year within less than three years.

■ **YORK**

In 1972, AMF's massive plant in York, Pennsylvania, lay almost idle. This coincided, after two decades in the doldrums, with Harley-Davidson's dire need for more manufacturing capacity and, not least, with one of

■ RIGHT *"The Tool",
a 70 year-old monster
which presses fuel
tanks at York.*

Milwaukee's periodic upsurges in union militancy. York was refurbished and motorcycle final assembly took over. The first "York" Harley rolled off the lines in February 1973. Capitol Drive would now build only engines and transmissions. York remains Harley's largest production facility, although production is less diverse than it once was. After buy-out, York continued to manufacture military

■ BELOW *Capitol Drive
now reconditions
customer engines.*

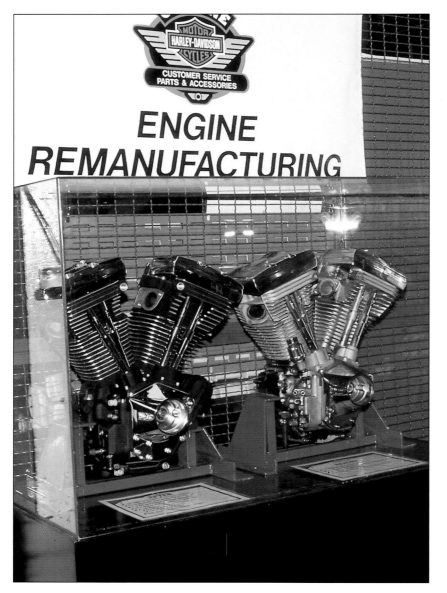

hardware – the casings on some of the bombs dropped over Iraq during the Gulf War were made at York – as well as IBM circuit boards. These peripheral activities have now ceased.

In common with the rest of the company, the plant at York has received massive investment in recent years – not the least of which was a new paint shop to unplug what was once the biggest production bottleneck.

With the transfer of Sportster production to Kansas, York now concentrates on building Big Twins on four lines – three for customs and one for heavyweight tourers.

■ TOMAHAWK, WISCONSIN
About 250 miles (402 km) north-west of Milwaukee lies the old Tomahawk boat company plant, of which Harley-Davidson bought a 60 per cent share in 1962. The 35,000sq ft (3,250sq metre) plant was purchased principally to make Servi-Car three-wheeler and golf-cart bodies (for which Harley-Davidson once controlled a third of the American market). It has since specialized in the manufacture of fairings, saddlebags, windshields and sidecars.

Like pretty much everywhere else in the Harley-Davidson empire, Tomahawk was

■ RIGHT *This plant on Pilgrim Road, Menomonee Falls was once the home of Briggs and Stratton engines, but has produced Harley "heavy powertrains" since 1997.*

recently expanded after an extension of 14,250sq ft (1,300sq metres) was completed in 1997.

■ **KANSAS CITY, MISSOURI**
The brand-new $85 million plant in Kansas City is the jewel in Harley's manufacturing crown. The first machines rolled off the line at the 330,000sq ft (30,000sq metre) factory in 1998. Kansas builds all Sportster models.

Kansas is the nearest Hog-building comes to state-of-the art. Expressions like "evolutionary turning point" and "ergonomically-friendly production lines" roll off corporate tongues as easily as "unique labour-management joint leadership philosophy".

■ **MILWAUKEE**
There was a time when "Milwaukee" meant just one thing – Juneau Avenue. Capitol Drive then opened to confuse the issue. Now there are six facilities in the Milwaukee area.

The Product Development Center (PDC) is where future H-D models are created. It is immediately behind the Capitol Drive engine

■ BELOW *Pilgrim Road is where the latest Twin Cam 88 and 88B engines are built.*

factory measuring 213,000sq ft (20,000sq metres), was completed in 1997 at a cost of $40 million.

In 1997, a new Big Twin powerline plant was opened in nearby Menomonee Falls, and a new P&A Distribution Centre at Franklin, outside Milwaukee.

Pilgrim Road now produces all Evo and Twin Cam engines, before final assembly at York. Buells are built a half-hour's drive to the south-west, in East Troy, Wisconsin.

Harley-Davidson hasn't witnessed such expansion since the First World War. Production for 1998 totalled 148,000 machines compared to just 62,000 at the start of the 1990s. Thanks to the impetus provided by Kansas, production is planned to increase even further in the near future.

All of this is a very long way away from that little wooden shed where it all began.

The Hardware

Wild innovation has never been the Milwaukee way. Neither young Bill Harley nor the Davidsons had a taste for the radical or the extreme. Almost from the outset, their target was dependability. That's not to say that Juneau Avenue was opposed to progress. In the pre-First World War years, Harley maintained a steady stream of technical novelties. By 1912, Harley-Davidson offered a choice of all-chain drive and a primitive clutch on the X8E model. The 1914 models boasted carburettor chokes, internally-expanding rear drum brakes and two-speed transmission. The first three-speed Harley appeared the following year, with a proper engine clutch.

Bill Harley was quick to understand the importance of heat-treatment and metallurgy, and quick to employ this new, unseen technology in his designs. Exotic alloy steels appeared inside even the first Milwaukee V-twins; similar developments occurred with frame construction and lubrication.

This tradition of rugged simplicity and steady improvement can be traced to the present day, through seven generations of classic V-twin engine. First came the inlet-over-exhaust and side-valve designs, followed by the revered Knucklehead, Panhead, Shovelhead and Evolution motors. By 1998, the latest in 90 years of big-inch V-twins, the Twin Cam, had graced the Milwaukee stage.

F-Heads & Flatheads

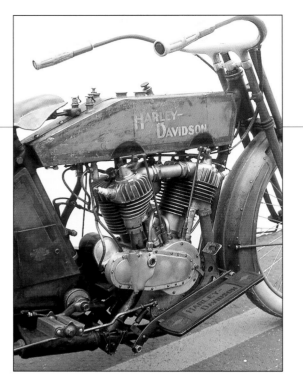

■ LEFT *The F-head.
The long push-rods to
the overhead inlet
valves and the "under
head" exhaust valves
are clear on the
1915 twin shown here.*

■ F-HEADS

A halfway house between flathead and overhead valve design was the inlet-over-exhaust (ioe) layout. Also called the "F-head", as the name suggests, this configuration combined an overhead inlet valve with a side exhaust valve.

All early Harleys followed this design, with one important additional characteristic. For reasons of simplicity, the inlet valve was of the "automatic" or induction type, in which the descending piston simply "sucks" the valve open only for it to be returned to its seat by a conventional spring. This spring was of necessity light, which precluded high engine revs. One major advantage of the system was that by removing the inlet valve housing, both valves could be removed easily for servicing – a considerable advantage on these relatively primitive engines. It was also found that since the valves directly faced each other, the incoming fuel charge helped cool the exhaust valve, extending its life. As well as the early singles, the first V-engines adopted the same

layout – to their cost, for it proved an untimely failure with the twin cylinder design.

Both the revised twin and the 5–35 series singles of 1913–18 moved to a far more positive ioe arrangement with a conventional, mechanically-operated overhead inlet valve. The same design was grafted on to the 74-inch Model J of 1922, also known as the "Super-powered Twin". This 18 horsepower engine was also the first Milwaukee twin to feature lightweight aluminium pistons. When Model J

■ LEFT *Inlet-over-
exhaust layout was the
norm on singles, such as
this 1914 example.*

production ended in 1929, Harley twins remained exclusively side-valvers for the next six years.

■ **FLATHEADS**

"Flathead" was the unflattering generic title given to any side-valve engine, whether made by Harley-Davidson or not. The reason for the nickname is obvious: with all the valve gear, including the valves themselves, located below the level of the piston at the top of its stroke, the heads were flat. The first side-valve Harleys were the Series A and B singles of 1926. All roadster twins from the end of the 1920s until the arrival of the Knucklehead in 1936 were flatheads as well. Milwaukee's catalogues continued to feature side-valve models until 1951 and even into the 1970s.

Side-valve engines were popular because they were relatively cheap to make and maintain, as well as much more compact than F-head and overhead valve designs. Although valve control was usually quite good – the camshaft and valves were in close proximity – the side-valve layout inevitably produced an elongated combustion chamber with tortuous gas-flow characteristics and poor valve cooling. This placed a severe limitation on the power such designs could produce. Side-valvers were renowned as dependable plodders, such as the seemingly unstoppable WL45.

■ ABOVE LEFT *By the late 1920s, side-valve engines were the norm.*

■ ABOVE RIGHT *Sidevalve engines formed the backbone of the Harley range into the 1950s, as with this WL45.*

■ BELOW *This angle clearly shows the utter simplicity of the basic side-valve V-twin.*

Harley's side-valve years threw up one notable exception, however – the overhead valve 21-inch (346cc) single, produced from 1926 until the eve of the Knuckle in 1935. Designed with the help of Harry Ricardo, this single was not only successful in its own right but gave rise to the celebrated "Peashooter" racer. Five years earlier, Ricardo created the Model R, Triumph's first four-valve engine. His company contributed to the development of the latest Triumph triples and Aprilia's new V-twin, the RSV Mille.

KNUCKLEHEAD, 1936–47

The Knucklehead's chunky looks make it the quintessential Harley-Davidson. To many motorcyclists its debut in 1936 announced the end of years of crippling economic depression survived by only two American motorcycle manufacturers – Harley and Indian. Sales were so poor that, only one year earlier, Harley's entire range comprised just two models. With the new model – formally designated the Model E – as its flagship, Harley's fortunes rapidly improved. Sales in 1937 exceeded 11,000 for the first time in the decade.

Development of what would become the Knuckle effectively began in the late 1920s, first with specials comprising single-cylinder Peashooter top-ends grafted on to existing V-twin JDH crankcases, then with the factory DAH racers. Although substantially new, the DAH utilized heads derived from the Peashooter's. Board approval for the "official" Knuckle project was granted in 1931 – a bold move at a time when the factory was running at just ten per cent capacity. The engine would probably have been in production by 1934 but for government

■ ABOVE *The Knucklehead, Harley's first production overhead valve twin.*

■ BELOW *Developed from the ohv Peashooter single, the Knuckle was a direct ancestor to the Evo engine of 1984.*

restrictions intended to reduce unemployment which effectively barred overtime in the engine development shop. It was a long haul but certainly worth the wait.

The Knuckle was a Juneau Avenue "first" in many respects – the first four (forward) speeder, the first engine with hemispherical (hemi) heads and the first overhead valve roadster twin. The engine was heavily influenced by the competition experience of the legendary Joe Petrali, Harley-Davidson development rider and near-unbeatable racer. The Knuckle announced its arrival with a resounding flourish by posting 136.183mph on the sands of Daytona Beach, Florida. This speed record still stands.

The 61-inch – actually 60.32cu in (989cc) – Knuckle was initially available in three specifications: E (standard), ES (sidecar) and EL (high compression sport, with 6.5:1 pistons). Petrali's influence was clear. With more than 40 horsepower at 4,800rpm, the EL in particular offered a huge increase in performance over the sluggish side-valvers. Despite its leisurely route to production – and not for the first time – there were initial reliability problems.

The worst of these concerned its new dry-sump lubrication. Some parts got too little oil while others – including the road underneath – got too much. A partial fix came in 1937 but the problem was not solved fully until the arrival of the 73.7cu in (1,207cc) Model F Knuckle in 1941, with its centrifugally-controlled oil pump by-pass. Although notorious for oil leaks through its many external seals and separate primary drive oiling, in very hot conditions many riders would prefer the big Knuckle's oil system to that of the later, "improved" Panhead.

■ ABOVE *But for the Depression, the Knucklehead would almost certainly have reached production before 1937.*

■ BELOW LEFT AND RIGHT *The numbers of Knuckelehead models built were severely curtailed by the Second World War, three years after which it was succeeded by the Panhead.*

The bigger Knucklehead had come about largely in response to competition from large-capacity Indian V-twins. The larger engine's extra torque demanded a new seven-plate clutch in place of the old five-plate device, giving 65 per cent greater friction area. In addition, there was a bigger rear brake, an "airplane-style" speedometer and a larger, more efficient air-cleaner.

For a variety of reasons, the Knuckle never quite made the impact it deserved. It would certainly have reached production earlier, but for the Depression. No sooner had the Model F reached the street than the Japanese attacked Pearl Harbor in December 1941. The outbreak of war obliged the factory to divert most of its attention to military production.

Milwaukee lore has it that the best of the big Knuckles were those built in that final pre-war year, but hostilities meant that relatively few 74-inch (1,207cc) Knuckles reached the road until 1947.

By 1948, a new boss at Harley meant that the Knuckle was consigned to the annals of company history.

PANHEAD, 1948–65

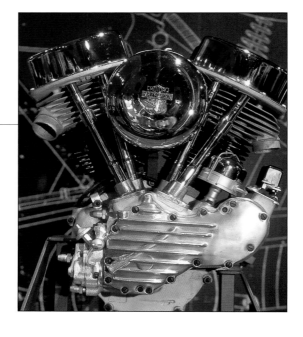

In 1945, Harley resumed civilian motorcycle production, although sales would not return to pre-war levels (partly due to industrial action) until 1947. In 1948, the replacement for the noble Knucklehead made its first public appearance.

In the Milwaukee tradition of steady evolution, the "Panhead", as it was dubbed, was a development of the Knuckle rather than an all-new concept. So-named because its chromed steel rocker covers (stainless steel from 1949) resembled inverted baking pans, the Pan was built in both 74-inch – actually 73.66cu in or 1,207cc – and 61-inch (989cc) sizes, although the latter was discontinued in 1953. The larger version retained the "traditional" bore and stroke dimensions of 3$\frac{7}{16}$ x 3$\frac{31}{32}$in (or 87.3 x 100.8mm).

The Pan featured aluminium alloy cylinder heads in place of the Knuckle's cast iron ones, new rocker gear and hydraulic tappets (or "lifters" as they're known in the United States)

■ BELOW LEFT *Since 1948 Pans have powered everything from the first Glide, the HydraGlide...*

■ BELOW RIGHT *...to crazy dirt racers, as pictured here.*

rather than noisier solid push-rods, as well as a revised and less leaky lubrication system. The camshaft was also new. Although the bottom-end was substantially like the Knuckle's, the oil system benefited from a larger capacity oil pump and the main oil feeds were now internal rather than untidy external lines.

The new aluminium heads not only improved engine cooling but contributed to an engine weight 8lbs (3.6kg) lighter than before. To ensure durability, the spark plugs and cylinder bolts threaded into steel inserts rather than the

■ RIGHT *The very first ElectraGlide was Panhead-powered.*

■ ABOVE FAR RIGHT *The DuoGlide had also been Panhead-powered.*

relatively soft aluminium of the head itself. Despite these improvements, the power output of early Pans was about the same as the Knuckle's – around 50bhp at 4,800rpm for the 74-inch motor. The valve lifters were relocated from the top of the push-rods in 1953, to lie between cam lobe and push-rod in the timing case. At the same time, both crankcase halves were heavily modified, with particular emphasis on oil control. In 1956, Harley-Davidson introduced even more of the same. By now, a freer-breathing air cleaner and high-

lift "Victory" camshaft had brought a gain of around 5bhp on the Pan's original power output. Near the end of its life in 1963, the Panhead reverted to the Knucklehead's external top-end oil feeds to prevent overheating, a particular problem in the scorching deserts of the American south-west.

At least as enduring as the Panhead itself was the name given to the first new model to bear such an engine.

The HydraGlide of 1949 was the first Harley-Davidson to employ hydraulically-damped telescopic front forks.
It was also the first model granted one of the enduring names in motorcycling: "Glide".

The Panhead engine would do much to get the famous species on its way, propelling not only the DuoGlide of 1958 but the very first of the ElectraGlides as well.

■ BELOW *One of the first Panhead Harleys, a 1948 girder-forked Model F.*

SHOVELHEAD, 1966–84

According to Harley lore, 1965 is notable for two things. The first was the unveiling of a new generation of Shovelhead engines, replacing the venerable Pans. Second and ultimately far more momentous was the decision to list the company on the stock market. What no doubt seemed a good idea at the time would ultimately lead to takeover by American Machine and Foundry (AMF).

Popular opinion now says that AMF neglected the company, that it didn't understand motorcycles and that quality went rapidly downhill. Much of this criticism has an element of truth to it but AMF actually sank millions of dollars into its new project and actually tripled annual sales.

If Harley had a problem it was probably as much to do with being part of America as being part of AMF for, like many other sectors of American industry, it was overwhelmed by the

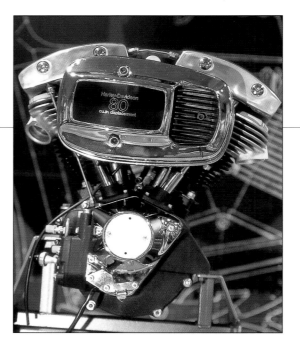

■ LEFT *Early Shovelheads used an all-new light alloy top end on what were essentially Panhead crankcases.*

tidal wave of sophisticated new products pouring in from Japan. As the British motorcycle industry learned to even greater cost, the 1960s and 1970s were no place for leisurely updates of a 1930s design. Put simply, the Shovelhead never had a chance.

First seen on the 1966 ElectraGlide, the Shovelhead followed the usual Harley practice of bolting a new top-end on to the tried-and-tested crankcases developed during the course of the previous generation of engines. There were minor revisions to the right crankcase half and a fin-less timing cover, but the bottom-end was essentially that of a 1965 Panhead, including the external oil feeds reintroduced in 1964.

An all-new top-end included aluminium alloy cylinder heads and iron cylinder barrels. Light alloy was also used for the rocker boxes in place of the Panhead's pressed steel. These were derived from the XL Sportster engine and enclosed redesigned rockers and exhaust valves. Although this rendered the Shovel top-end slightly reminiscent of the Sportster range, the latter was a quite separate family of unit-construction engines. Equally striking was the Shovel's "Ham-can" air cleaner cover, mated to a constant velocity Tillotson diaphragm carb from late 1966 onwards. The "Power Pac" head

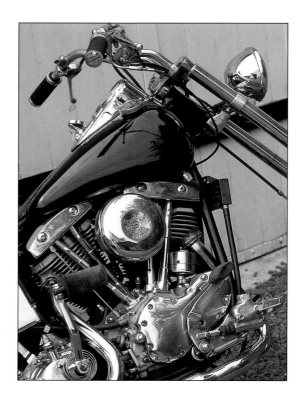

■ FAR LEFT *This is a "generator" Shovelhead, produced up to 1970.*

and one reverse). The Shovel received its new bottom-end in 1970, in which a crankshaft-mounted alternator replaced the previous generator (and made the engine even wider) — hence "generator" and "alternator" Shovels. The later type, also called "cone motors", are recognized by their cone-shaped, right-side engine cover. The ignition points assembly was moved from its original external position inside the timing case and the timing gears simplified.

Originally produced in 74cu in (1,207cc) form, Shovels grew to 80cu in (1,340cc) with the FLH-80 of 1978, when electronic ignition was added. Two years later, the first five-speed gearbox appeared, firstly on the FLT Tour-Glide, and was also the first of Harley's rubber-mounted engines.

design gave around 60bhp in FLH specification, 5bhp more than an equivalent Panhead. The standard FL developed 54bhp. Observers described the new heads as resembling the backs of coal shovels, hence the nickname.

Like all Harley Vs, the ohv engine runs forked con-rods with both cylinders in the same plane to eliminate rocking couple. Primary drive is via chain to a four-speed box (with a sidecar option up to 1980, of three forward

■ BELOW *"Alternator" Shovelheads are recognizable by the conical housing on the end of the crankshaft, here marked with AMF's Number One logo.*

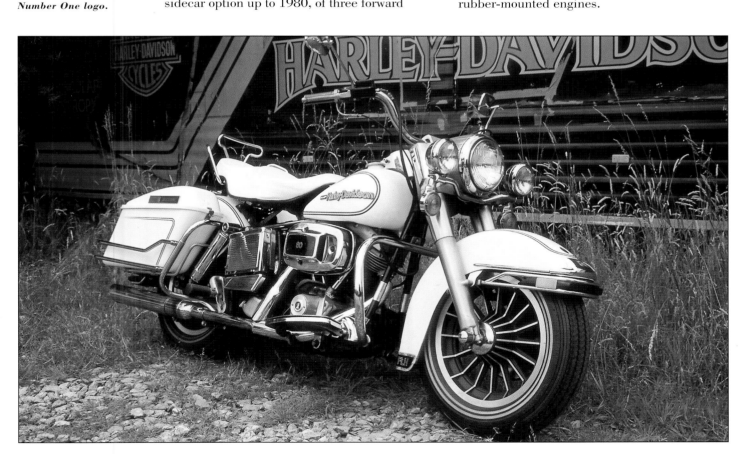

V2 EVOLUTION, 1984–PRESENT

Perhaps the biggest fault of the next in Milwaukee's noble line of big twins is the lack of an attractive nickname. Its official title is "V2 Evolution" which, in common with most Milwaukee monikers, is a registered trademark. It is also profoundly fitting, since like the Shovel and Panhead before, it evolved from its predecessor rather than representing an all-new design.

Appropriate as the name might be, it is not evocative at all. After decades of Flatheads, Knuckles, Pans and Shovels, it has to be said that "Evo" lacks the same gritty authentic ring. Happily for its creators, an unkind early suggestion of "Blockhead" failed to stick.

It's a curious Milwaukee fact that all major Harley-Davidson ohv engines have been born in the midst of strife. The Knuckle was a child of the Depression, the Pan arrived surrounded by strikes and post-war rebuilding, and the Shovel heralded years of decline. As the long-

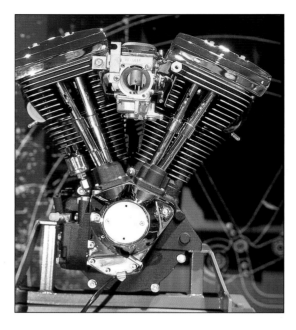

awaited replacement for the Shovel arrived in 1984, Harley-Davidson was effectively broke. The story of how the company got out of perhaps the biggest crisis in its history is

■ LEFT *The Evolution engine was developed from the Shovelhead twin, but soon proved itself stronger, cleaner and more dependable. It saved Harley's fortunes just in time.*

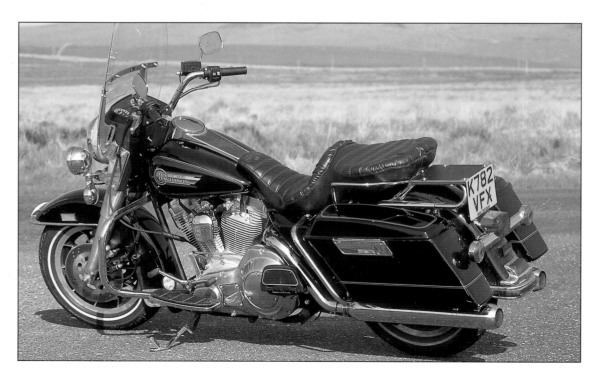

■ LEFT *By 1985, Evolution engines powered the entire big twin range, with Sportsters getting similar treatment one year later. It eventually gave way to the Twin Cam.*

■ RIGHT *The Fat Boy is one of the most stylish examples of the Softail family.*

related elsewhere, but never was Milwaukee in greater need of an engine that would deliver the goods for them.

Fortunately for Harley-Davidson fans everywhere, the Evo was – and remains – everything they and Milwaukee had hoped for. Compared to the venerable Shovel which began life 18 years before, the Evo is 20lbs (9kgs) lighter and generates 10 per cent more horsepower and 15 per cent more torque. Its cylinders retain the "classic" dimensions of $3\frac{7}{16}$ x $4\frac{1}{4}$in (88.8 x 108mm), giving an actual displacement of 81.8cu in or 1,340cc (not 80in as it is nominally called). As with the evolution of Pan to Shovel, the Evo uses a bottom-end derived from its (alternator-type) predecessor but with improved con-rods and a new all-alloy top end. Efforts were made to improve oil-tightness and reliability, and decrease maintenance chores, with great success.

The extra power (around 70bhp at 5,000rpm) comes mainly from steeper, straighter ports feeding into redesigned combustion chambers, a new ignition, revised valve timing and higher compression ratios. During the seven years of the new engine's

development, much effort also went into redesigning the lubrication system to prevent the Shovel's notoriously leaky nature. All but a handful of Evos sport five-speed transmission and, from later 1984, a much-improved diaphragm clutch. By 1986, the 1340 Evo had been joined by V2 Sportster cousins offering 883cc and 1100cc, the latter growing to become the first 1200cc Sportster two years later. Unlike the 1340s, Sportster Evos are of unit construction in which the crankcases and gearbox form a single unit.

So much for metal. As far as the vibrant, imaginative management team running the newly-independent company was concerned, the Evo had one other priceless asset the much-derided Shovelhead lacked. Milwaukee now seemed to have its finger on the pulse of motorcycle culture, and most importantly, seemed to understand its market.

Those at the helm now reached out to their customers in a way that the remote, faceless AMF never could, in stark contrast to the Shovelhead era. They sold their new product as if Harley's life depended on it – which, make no mistake, it did.

TWIN CAM 88

The Twin Cam was unveiled in 1998 and billed as "the biggest change in engine design since the Knuckle". First seen on the 1999 SuperGlides, DynaGlides, Road Kings, RoadGlide and ElectraGlide, the Twin Cam offers more power and torque in a smoother, more refined package. Yet despite the name, this is still an overhead valve engine – the cams in question are downstairs. Unlike the gear-driven camshafts of previous big twins, these are chain-driven and far less costly to produce. Considerable savings are also made in crankcase machining, which required 37 distinct operations on the Evo but only three on the Twin Cam.

One area which received particular attention was the oil circulation. Surprising though it may seem, as they set out to create the Twin Cam, Milwaukee's engineers had very little idea what the lubricating oil in the Evo engine actually did – except that it didn't always go where it ought and that pressure could fall dangerously under very hot conditions. After 18 months of painstaking work on engines littered with Plexiglass "windows", the engineers believed they had the new engine figured out at last. In fact, the actual hardware

■ RIGHT *Known as plain P22 during development, the Twin Cam has yet to attract a pet name, despite unkind suggestions that "Fat head" might fit the bill.*

– a high-capacity "gerotor" pump and two distinct scavenge systems – is less crucial than the engine's internal detailing. This was simple compared to the project's biggest problem, which had nothing to do with hardware, but with people. After the lay-offs of the 1980s, Harley simply didn't have a team capable of developing a new engine. One had to be created almost from scratch before work on the Twin Cam could begin.

■ BELOW *The Twin Cam brought a new dimension of power and refinement, first to heavyweight Glides, then the Softail range.*

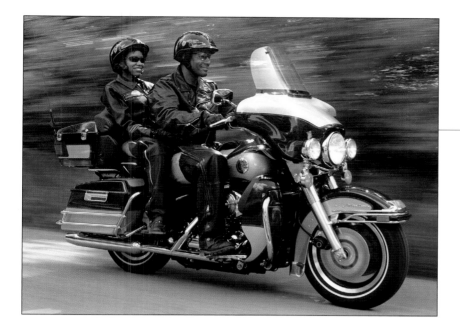

■ ABOVE *Faster,
cleaner, easier to
service–any Harley
rider's delight.*

Depending on the state of tune, Harley claims a
14–22 per cent power increase (to 87bhp on the
DynaGlides) compared to the previous
Evolution design. This is achieved partly
through higher compression ratios, improved
combustion-chamber shape and induction
plumbing, as well as a new ignition pack.

Last but not least is a ten per cent increase in
capacity to 88.4cu in (1,449cc), making this
the largest stock engine Milwaukee has ever
built. To achieve the extra volume, the stroke
has decreased from 4¼ to 4in (108 to 101.6mm)
while the bore has risen substantially from
3⅞ to 3¹³⁄₁₆ (88.8 to 95.3mm). Traditionalists

may bemoan the departure from the hallowed
88.8 x 108mm (3⅞ x 4¼in) dimensions which
have endured since the Shovel.

They will certainly not bemoan, however, the
Twin Cam's prodigious peak torque: 86lb/ft
(116Nm) at a mere 3,500rpm. Riders needing
more can take heart: the Twin Cam was designed
to allow an increase in displacement as high as
1550cc, adding another six to eight horsepower.

Compared to the bolted-up crankshafts of
previous ohv twins, the Twin Cam has a
pressed-up crankshaft. With its shorter stroke,
it is capable of higher revs. Although the
5,500rpm redline is only 300rpm higher than
before, development engines have been safely
tested at up to 7,000rpm.

Harley surprised everyone by dropping the
Evo and unveiling the Twin Cam 88B for the
year 2000, a unit-construction engine
specifically tailored for the Softail range.

It represents another Harley first – twin
balance-shafts to smooth out engine vibrations.
Softails will no longer be able to lay claim to
being the "judderers" of the range.

■ RIGHT *Twin Cam
power reached the
Softail range with the
balance-shafted Twin
Cam 88B for year-
2000 models.*

RETRO-TECH

Harley-Davidson, like any ambitious pioneer motorcycle company in its early years, introduced scores of new ideas and technologies as its motorized bicycles evolved into true motorcycles. With running gear, as with engines, change was based on a trial-and-error philosophy, in which good practice prospered and bad quickly failed and fell into disuse. It was soon clear to Harley-Davidson's founders, however, that their interests lay foremost in making things that worked – and dependably. Unfamiliar ground was broached only in response to some specific need or shortcoming, and then with a thoroughness that often escaped their rivals. To this extent, the company has changed little.

It's perhaps surprising, then, that Juneau Avenue occasionally lapsed into dubious claims of motorcycling "firsts". The "step-start" and front brake, introduced in 1914 and

1927 respectively, are cases in point. British Scotts had kick-starts much earlier and front brakes were already commonplace on European machines by the 1920s. In 1923, for instance, Douglas racers were sporting quite modern-looking front-disc brakes. When Harley-Davidson claimed a "first", what it really meant was an American first.

Milwaukee makes little pretence at space-age technological innovation these days, although it might claim its machines are state-

■ ABOVE *Even today, all Harleys use variations of twin-loop steel frames, as on this one on the York assembly line.*

■ FAR LEFT AND LEFT *Two of Milwaukee's major innovations: belt final drive, as on this five-speed 883 Sportster (far left) and the "Retro-Tech" Springer front end (left).*

of-the-art – with the emphasis very much on "art". In sheer performance terms, novel engineering is usually introduced slowly: its first five-speed gearbox in 1980; fuel injection in 1995 (to clean up emissions more than to enhance power); and the long-awaited and still anticipated overhead cams (other than on the high-tech VR1000 Superbike racer). The two fields in which Harley-Davidson has taken a lead are in toothed-belt final drive – a relatively simple but truly wonderful development first seen on the 1980 FXB Sturgis – and, most strikingly, the concept of "Retro-Tech".

Retro-Tech grew out of the imaginations of Willie G. Davidson and his colleagues at the Product Development Center as well as the ingenuity of Harley's engineers. It is the means by which modern engineering receives a post-modern styling twist which is uniquely Harley-Davidson, which can contrive to make a 1999 model look for all the world like a 1949 HydraGlide but function far better. Willie G. coined the phrase, the "New Nostalgia".

Its chief elements are the Springer and Softail front and rear ends, respectively. The Softail system, designed by consulting engineer Bill Davis and much imitated by

■ ABOVE *Another view of the Springer front forks, inspired by the girder forks of Harleys of the 1940s.*

■ BELOW *Detail of the revolutionary Sturgis of 1991.*

■ LEFT *This deceptively simple-looking rubberized mounting transformed the ride of the 1993 WideGlide and subsequent Dyna-Glide models.*

competitors, comprises a cantilever suspension system using two underslung shock absorbers cunningly persuaded to look like the rigid rear end of bygone days. Hence the name – Softail, a play on the "hard tail" nickname of custom machines whose rear suspension has been removed in favour of lines that are cleaner, if distinctly less comfortable.

Springer front forks are highly-stylized facsimiles of the girder forks used on Harleys prior to the HydraGlide. Despite the 1940s looks created by their exposed springs and brilliant chrome blades, Springer forks benefited from more computer-aided design than any previous piece of Harley-Davidson hardware had done.

Almost any other make of motorcycle you can mention boasts "more" than any Harley-Davidson – more cylinders, valves and camshafts, more gears, more revs, more power – but with Milwaukee's finest, as the cognoscenti well understand, less is more.

If a Harley is about anything, it's about getting back to motorcycling's roots. As styling vice president Willie G. himself observed a few years ago, owners "rank the Harley look right up there with motherhood and God and they don't want us to screw around with it." Like that other American icon, the Zippo cigarette lighter, "It Works".

And, as the saying goes, "if it ain't broke, don't try to fix it."

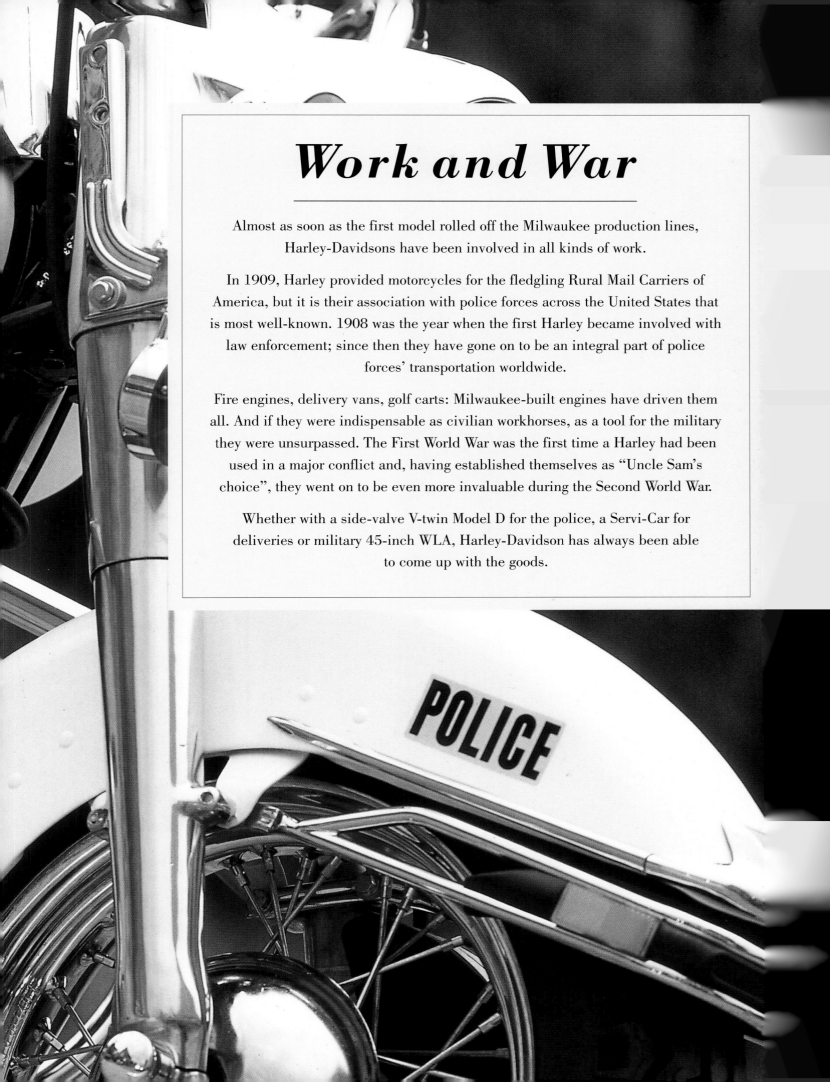

Work and War

Almost as soon as the first model rolled off the Milwaukee production lines, Harley-Davidsons have been involved in all kinds of work.

In 1909, Harley provided motorcycles for the fledgling Rural Mail Carriers of America, but it is their association with police forces across the United States that is most well-known. 1908 was the year when the first Harley became involved with law enforcement; since then they have gone on to be an integral part of police forces' transportation worldwide.

Fire engines, delivery vans, golf carts: Milwaukee-built engines have driven them all. And if they were indispensable as civilian workhorses, as a tool for the military they were unsurpassed. The First World War was the first time a Harley had been used in a major conflict and, having established themselves as "Uncle Sam's choice", they went on to be even more invaluable during the Second World War.

Whether with a side-valve V-twin Model D for the police, a Servi-Car for deliveries or military 45-inch WLA, Harley-Davidson has always been able to come up with the goods.

WORK AND WAR

■ WORK

Throughout the 1920s and 1930s, the words "Harley-Davidson" and "workhorse" were almost synonymous. Surprising though it may seem now, much of America's road network scarcely existed until President Roosevelt's job-creation programmes of the Depression years. Even the celebrated Route 66 dates from only 1926 (and was almost obliterated by Interstate 40 after 1985). Any affordable, rugged machine able to cope with rough terrain had something going for it, and Milwaukee's finest certainly met that bill. Harleys have offered mobility in every walk of American life, from painters to policemen. The company saw this potential early – Arthur Davidson attended the annual meeting of the Rural Mail Carriers of America as early as 1909, coming away with a pocketful of sales. It is with the police, however, especially the Highway Patrol, that Milwaukee twins are best associated.

Literally thousands of Harleys have joined America's police forces since they first went into uniform in 1908. Until recently, it was believed that the first police Harley went to Pittsburgh in 1909, although the distinction actually goes to Detroit one year earlier. Indeed, Harley-Davidsons have been popular across the globe, and Milwaukee twins have often been prominent in newsreel footage of presidential cavalcades in countries as far-flung as Burma and Guatemala. By 1915, Juneau Avenue was also producing "rapid response" sidecar outfits equipped with fire extinguishers and first-aid kits. A decade later, Harley motorcycles were in use by more than 2,500 American police forces, some of which quickly saw the public-relations benefits of organizing their riders into display teams. By the 1930s, police-model special equipment

■ ABOVE *Police officers on 1944 UL models patrol Minneapolis, Minnesota. Harleys have been involved in law enforcement since 1908.*

■ BELOW LEFT *The Servi-Car three-wheeler did much to allow Harley to endure the Depression.*

■ BELOW RIGHT *A police Panhead, one of thousands of machines to have served US law-enforcement.*

■ ABOVE *An impressive line-up of police Harleys outside the Juneau Avenue factory.*

included radios (initially only one-way; two-way arrived 1948), although some squads made riders buy their own police lights and sirens.

The same period also welcomed two definitive Harley-Davidson workhorses. The archetypal side-valve V-twin Model D, introduced in 1929, became the Model W in

■ RIGHT AND BELOW *This immaculately restored Flathead served with the Daytona Beach Fire Department.*

1937 and continued in production until 1951. Although crude and slow – its 22-or-so-bhp, 45-inch engine generated around 65mph (105kph) – it was rugged, dependable and easy to fix – ideal for cash-strapped Depression America. The American military version, known as the WLA – the "A" stood for "Army" – represented the bulk of Milwaukee's contribution to the Second World War. Though the majority of WL production during the war years was earmarked for military use, some also went to police forces and other strategic or security operations.

The Servi-Car, introduced for 1932, was the Model D's three-wheeled sister ship, and enjoyed an even longer production run – until 1974. The model's capacious boot (trunk) made it as popular with trade and delivery men as it was with local police forces. This unique three-wheeler remained in service, even in metropolitan San Francisco, into the 1990s. One clever and user-friendly Servi-Car touch was the adoption of the same 42in (1,070mm) wheelbase as the typical car – so inexperienced riders would not need to forge their own ruts in mud and snow.

So enduring was the Servi-Car's appeal that for a period during the late 1970s and early 1980s it was the only Milwaukee machine serving many American police forces.

The later Shovelhead years were not happy ones for Harley-Davidson's law-enforcing pretensions. Quality-control problems and general performance issues caused many forces to look elsewhere. For around a decade, even the California Highway Patrol (CHiPs) found itself powered by Italian Moto Guzzi V-twin and Japanese Kawasaki four-cylinder machines. It was not until the arrival of the Evolution engine in 1984 that Harley could again supply machinery that met CHiPs' requirements. Since then, Harley's principal police models have been the FLHT-P Electra-Glide and FXRP PursuitGlide.

■ THE FIRST WORLD WAR

By the time the United States entered the First World War in 1917, H-D machines had already seen action in skirmishes against the forces of Pancho Villa, the Mexican revolutionary. Under

General "Black Jack" Pershing, machine-gun-toting Harley-Davidsons proved themselves ideal for border patrols in rough terrain.

In the process, Juneau Avenue proved itself adept at meeting military demands. An order for additional machines was placed by a War Department telegraph on 16 March 1916. A

■ ABOVE LEFT *Fancy being paid to ride a Harley at Sturgis: a local cop.*

■ ABOVE RIGHT *Busted for good taste? Harley catches Harley.*

■ LEFT *An Evo serving with Volusia County Police, one of several forces in the Daytona Beach area.*

■ LEFT *Since the first police Harley of 1908 there have been literally thousands, most of which have travelled further than this.*

dozen motorcycles equipped with William Harley's design for a sidecar gun carriage duly arrived at the border – more than 1,000 miles (1,610km) distant – two days later. Nine days later still, a second order for six machines reached Milwaukee. This one was filled in just 33 hours. Needless to say, the factory was not slow to advertise its efficiency in meeting "Uncle Sam's Choice".

Harley was just as quick to recognize the contribution it might make to the war in Europe. Within four months of the United States' entry into the war, Arthur Davidson was telling a sales meeting where the country's – and perhaps the company's – destiny lay:

"The time is coming when no man can be in the middle of the road. He must be either for America or against America, and the sooner we get together on this question, the better able we will be to win the war."

During the first year of America's war, roughly half of all motorcycle production went to military service. By the end of the conflict, every motorcycle Milwaukee made was built for Uncle Sam. Along the way, William Harley, a member of the Motorcycle War Service Board, was instrumental in giving motorcycles a "B-4" classification, which gave them essential production status with priority for raw materials. Some 312 Harley-Davidson employees also enlisted, of whom all but three survived the experience.

As to hardware, in all some 20,000 motorcycles became American "conscripts" in the First World War, the vast majority of which were Harley-Davidsons. This success finally

■ ABOVE *Daytona: Sun, sea and Harleys.*

■ RIGHT *William Harley oversees the testing of specially equipped Harley twins during the early years of the First World War.*

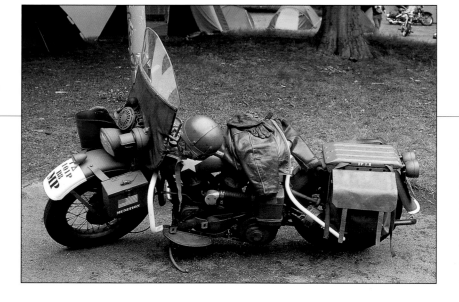

leap-frogged Harley ahead of its main rival, Indian, a position it was never to relinquish. Military Harleys were mainly 61-inch (989cc) twins of conventional F-head design, producing almost nine horsepower. They were employed mainly for dispatch and scout duty. One became a cause célèbre.

Its rider was Corporal Roy Holtz of Chippewa Falls, Wisconsin, little more than 200 miles (320 km) from downtown Milwaukee. On 8 November 1918, with the German army in chaotic retreat, Holtz was assigned to take his company captain on a reconnaissance mission. At night and in foul weather, the captain became disorientated and, over Holtz's objections, directed him across enemy lines where the duo eventually stumbled across a German field headquarters at which Holtz was instructed to ask directions. They were taken prisoner but released with the Armistice three days later. Holtz – and his Harley V-twin – thus became the first American serviceman on German soil.

■ THE SECOND WORLD WAR

No sooner had Harley sales begun to recover from the Depression of the 1930s than Pearl Harbor was bombed and the United States entered the Second World War. Milwaukee had begun planning in anticipation of military needs as early as the autumn of 1939, shortly

■ ABOVE *A Second World War WLA45 assigned to the US military police.*

after the outbreak of war in Europe. Early work, in competition with Indian and Delco, focused on a flat twin Servi-Car to meet army proposals for a three-wheeler for rough terrain. Other unfinished projects were even stranger, including an armoured machine-gun carrier and a prototype powerplant for a small tank comprising paired overhead valve engines.

With civilian motorcycle production suspended, by far the bulk of Harley-Davidson's war effort was the production of military versions of the WL side-valve V-twins, the WLA. The equivalent 74-inch (1,207cc) military UA and USA (sidecar) models were built in much smaller numbers. Of almost 90,000 military Harley-Davidsons, around 88,000 were 45-inch WLAs, of which one third served with Soviet forces. The same attributes of rugged simplicity that had brought the side-valve twin such a dependable peacetime reputation made it ideally suited to the harsher demands of war.

With very few Knuckleheads "enlisting" (although a special ELC model was built for the Canadian army), Milwaukee's other major contribution was the oddball Model XA, powered by a horizontally-opposed flathead twin displacing 45cu in (739cc). The XA was

■ RIGHT *A particularly war-torn WLA, but they were remarkably sturdy machines.*

■ RIGHT *The horizontally-opposed XA twin looked more like a German BMW or Zundapp, but served in small numbers during the Second World War.*

expressly designed for use in the North African desert, with its shaft final drive and plunger rear suspension. There was also an XS variant, with sidecar. Less well known was a mission for American intelligence, the stripping and assessment of a Russian motorcycle.

Harley-Davidson's contribution was not confined to hardware. John E. Harley, later in charge of the parts and accessories division, rose to the rank of major in the Second World War. Among his various tasks, and one to which

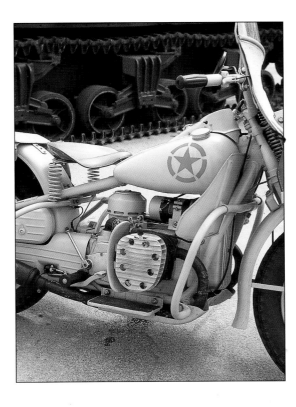

■ RIGHT *Although intended primarily for service in the North African desert – hence this colour scheme – the XA suffered badly from all the sand which would collect in its wheel bearings.*

he was eminently suited, was the training of army motorcyclists at Fort Knox, Kentucky. WLAs in the hands of raw recruits must have tested Harley's talents to the limit. Even setting off on such a machine was a knack, thanks to its hand gear-change and foot-operated "suicide" clutch.

From late 1941 until the armistice in 1945, Juneau Avenue burned the midnight oil to meet the escalating demands of the forces as almost the whole of American industry was turned over to the war effort. Fittingly, Harley-Davidson's special contribution was recognized by the award of three coveted Army-Navy "E" awards for excellence in wartime production. Milwaukee's factory workers couldn't necessarily go to war with the enemy but they could certainly help those who did.

Some might believe Harley's military career ended with the Second World War but there are two surprising post-scripts.

The first was the 1987 purchase of the rights to the military MT500 motorcycle from the British Armstrong company.

The second was a legacy of the AMF takeover: one "sideline" at the former AMF plant in York, Pennsylvania – where Harleys are still assembled – was the manufacture of bomb casings, a practice which continued well into the 1990s. It is likely that some of these found their way into the Gulf War.

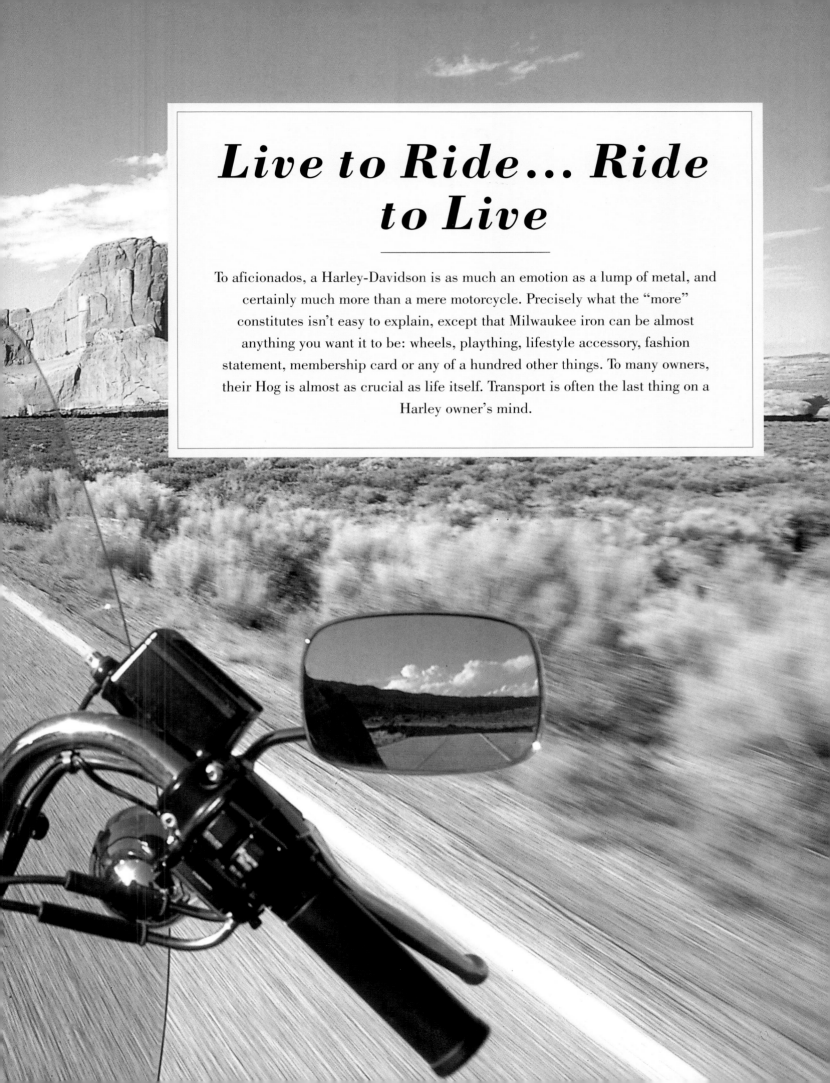

Live to Ride... Ride to Live

To aficionados, a Harley-Davidson is as much an emotion as a lump of metal, and certainly much more than a mere motorcycle. Precisely what the "more" constitutes isn't easy to explain, except that Milwaukee iron can be almost anything you want it to be: wheels, plaything, lifestyle accessory, fashion statement, membership card or any of a hundred other things. To many owners, their Hog is almost as crucial as life itself. Transport is often the last thing on a Harley owner's mind.

🏍 STYLE

The image forged from steel in the American Midwest travels across frontiers and media. It's as instantly recognizable in Bangkok as it is in Brooklyn, as rich with associations in Clackmannanshire as it is in Cincinnati. Advertisers know this and use it as shorthand for youth, freedom, rebellion and freewheeling affluence. It is almost impossible to watch a commercial for anything from cars and pensions to jeans and toiletries without a Harley-Davidson cropping up sooner or later in a mood-setting role. In other words, Harleys may be motorcycles – but they're also stars.

Some of this rubs off on the people who ride them. Owning a Harley isn't about speed or performance, or about imitating your favourite racer or impressing friends. It's about individuality but also brotherhood, retro-cool and happening places, latter-day cowboys or folk who just want to get away from it all.

When they move, Harley-Davidsons cruise. To the ear, they also thunder rather than rev.

You can cruise around the block, along the beach or down to the bar; equally you can cruise from New York to San Francisco if that's your thing. They work equally well on the long-haul because of where they evolved – in a land of empty spaces and almost no corners at all.

■ ABOVE *Poster of Peter Fonda and Dennis Hopper cruising to New Orleans in* Easy Rider.

■ LEFT *Christian Slater and Harley in* Heathers.

■ BELOW LEFT *"Captain America" and helmet, as ridden by Peter Fonda.*

■ BELOW *"Harley-Davidstones" – one Stones fan wears his heart on his Harley.*

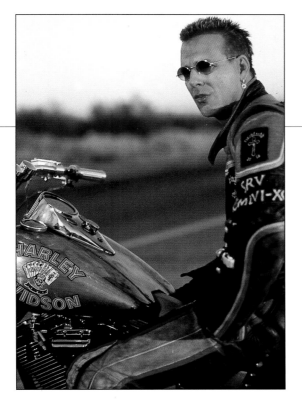

■ **LEFT** *Mickey Rourke cuts loose on a Harley in The Marlboro Man.*

■ **ABOVE** *You will find Hogs everywhere!*

■ BEAUTIFUL PEOPLE

"God rides a Harley", according to some. The King certainly rode one. As well as Elvis Presley, celebrity hoggers have included Muhammad Ali, Bob Dylan, Clint Eastwood, Sly Stallone, Mickey Rourke, Dan Ackroyd, Malcolm Forbes, Cher, Whoopie Goldberg and dozens more. You're as likely to see a film star

in Hollywood riding a Harley-Davidson today as lounging in a stretch limousine. Often, the stars want something out of the ordinary. Custom builders can easily charge $40,000 for bespoke machines and, in the process, become minor celebrities themselves.

The phenomenon is far from new, especially in Tinseltown. Photographs from Hollywood's golden years show everyone from *Gone with the Wind*'s Clark Gable to Marlene Dietrich astride Milwaukee machines. In some cases, the pictures were pure publicity stunts, but even Roy Rogers rode a Harley when he wasn't riding Trigger. Hollywood even had its own Harley group once – the Three Point Motorcycle Club.

Harleys themselves have become film stars, notably Robert Blake's mount in *Electra Glide in Blue* and, of course, in the hugely successful *Easy Rider* starring Dennis Hopper. Hopper's co-star in the film, Peter Fonda, remains a committed Harley-Davidson fan to this day.

■ **ABOVE** *"Made in the USA" – and long before Springsteen sang it.*

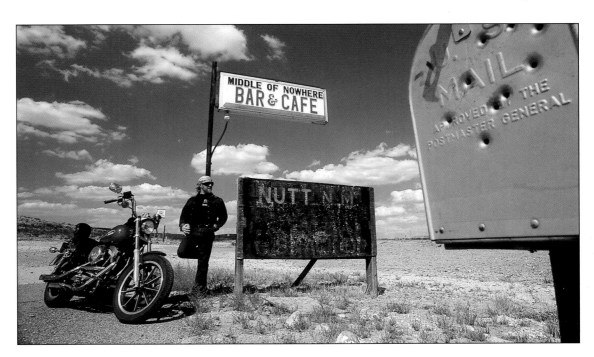

■ **RIGHT** *Nothing else out there: just you, your Harley and the open road.*

RALLIES: STURGIS

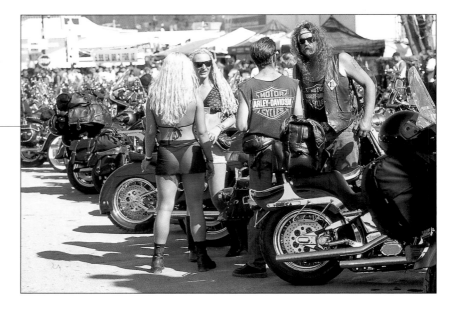

Sturgis is an unremarkable little farming community in South Dakota. For most of the year very little happens until, in mid-August, this sleepy little hamlet goes motorcycle crazy as the famous Sturgis Rally lets rip.

The monster that Sturgis has become was born way back in 1938 when the Jackpine Gypsies Motorcycle Club organized the first Black Hills Rally and Races, with a $300 purse to the winner. Almost every year since, bikers by the thousand have cruised in along Interstates 85 and 90 to renew old friendships or make new ones. Being conveniently located in middle America – if 900 miles (1,450 km) from Chicago and 1,500 miles (2,410 km) from San Francisco can be considered convenient – attendance tends to be huge. Any old Sturgis Rally attracts 50,000 of the faithful. For the 50th anniversary in 1990, somewhere between 250,000 and 300,000 turned up.

Sturgis is not specifically a Harley rally – not that you'd notice if you were there for all the Harley bikes on site. It lasts for a week – a week of swap meets, hog roasts (pigs, not bikes), drag-bike racing at the Sturgis Dragway, tours, gawking at fancy Harley hardware and generally having a good time. Bikers hang out at joints like the Bear Butte Café. Main Street is air-cleaner to wheel-spindle full of Hogs. If you need a break, there are tours to the nearby Dakota Badlands, Devil's Tower (featured in the movie *Close Encounters of the Third Kind*) or Mount Rushmore.

There's strangeness, as well. One year, a guy rode a buffalo into town, moseyed down Main Street and hung a left on to Junction Avenue. Another year, the nearby US Air Force base

■ ABOVE *At Sturgis, you don't necessarily need a lot of clothes, but they have to be the right ones.*

■ BELOW LEFT *Usually the action lasts right through the night.*

■ BELOW RIGHT *And some people say all Harley owners are alike.*

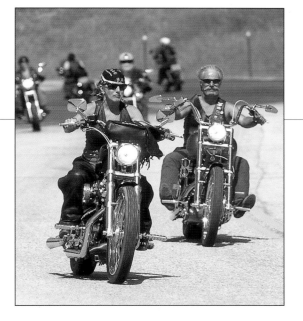

■ RIGHT *Ladies are welcome, too.*

■ BELOW *Main Street in Sturgis, as can be seen, is a car-free zone.*

reputedly laid on a rather special kind of fire-works display when a couple of their jets dipped low over town, hit their afterburners and drowned out even the noise of a thousand V-twins.

The whole town joins in (Sturgis is usually quite lucrative, although the town is so outnumbered by bikers it has little choice) from the women of the United Presbyterian to the Grace Lutherans. There have been occasional troubles with biker gangs, notably in 1982, but on the whole Sturgis is comparatively peaceful (if far from tranquil). These gangs are actively encouraged by the Sturgis city fathers, who clearly know a good deal when they see one.

According to Jackpine founder, former Indian dealer J.C. "Pappy" Hoel, there's never been a serious problem with outlaw biker groups: "We have their co-operation as long as we don't hassle them."

Mainly, it's a week-long party. Behaviour has been known to be on the excessive side, but it's usually harmless and only takes place once a year. Besides, it's legendary.

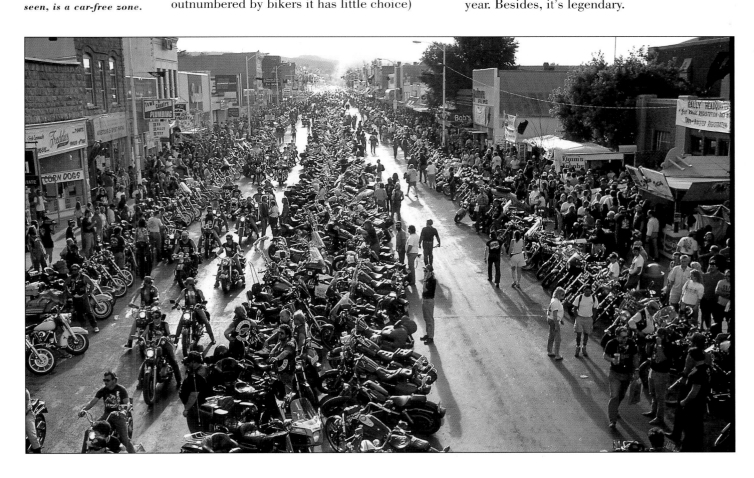

RALLIES: DAYTONA CYCLE WEEK

■ BELOW *Like it says: "Daytona Beach Welcomes Bikers".*

Outside the Rat's Hole custom shop, Main Street reverberates to the rumble of big-bore Vs on open pipes. Heavy-looking bikers in wraparound shades stand beergut-to-beergut, shoulder-to-tattooed-shoulder on every inch of sidewalk. It's March and almost 200,000 bikers have Daytona Beach under siege.

Like Sturgis, this is a week-long party. For the most part, the siege is friendly. As the barmaid at La Playa Hotel put it, "Bike Week's the best because they're all really nice. You don't see manners like this any other time. Wannanother beer?"

■ BADASS BIKERS?

Like Sturgis, Daytona's Cycle Week is one of those mammoth events that didn't begin as a celebration of all that is Harley-Davidson but somehow became one. Cycle Week takes place each year during March's Spring Break in the Florida coastal city of Daytona Beach. Its focal point is ostensibly the races at nearby Daytona International Speedway, a spectacular banked oval which also hosts the famous Daytona Nascar races.

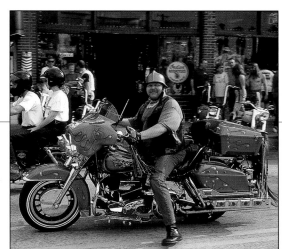

■ ABOVE LEFT *At Daytona you can cruise or watch others cruising...*

■ ABOVE RIGHT *...or you can just chill and chew the fat.*

It's yet another of those Harley enigmas that, as the factory's twins' interest in the races has declined, its profile in Cycle Week as a whole has risen dramatically. Milwaukee's official XR750 road racer last competed there in 1973 (although the VR1000 has competed in recent years) and hasn't had a win since Cal Rayborn's in 1969, but this hasn't spoiled the party one bit. Quite the reverse – not having to ride the few miles out to the Speedway seems to leave more time for downtown fun. Daytona has become pure festival.

Sturgis, a small town, is understandably overwhelmed by bikes. Daytona Beach is big, yet the effect is much the same. The scene centres on the junction of Atlantic and Main Street, where bikes and bodies are crammed sidewalk to sidewalk. Harley-Davidson – wise

to the public relations coup Daytona has handed them – takes over the city's Hilton Hotel to strut its corporate stuff and show the latest models. However most Daytona life goes on in the street, in the bars, on the beach and in nearby campgrounds.

Cycle Week has custom shows and impromptu drag races. During the day, bikes cruise along Daytona's beaches. There's official racing at the local quarter-mile dirt track and the main event at the International Speedway. There are swap meets in which enthusiasts sell or search for bike parts, notably at the Volusia County Fairgrounds.

Mainly it's lots of partyin', posin' and cruisin', and if you can't wait 12 months for your next Daytona fix, you can show up at the HOG "Biketoberfest" in October.

■ OPPOSITE BELOW LEFT *Spot the Honda.*

■ OPPOSITE BELOW RIGHT *If you can find a standard bike, you can keep it.*

■ RIGHT *If you can't paint your Hog, paint your clothes...*

■ FAR RIGHT *...if there's anything left to paint, that is.*

BAD BOYS

Mention Harley-Davidson to anyone in the street and they'll probably mutter back something about "Hell's Angels". The original Angels were a California bike gang of Second World War veterans sensationalized by magazines such as Life and author Hunter S. Thompson in his book *The Hell's Angels: A Strange and Terrible Saga of the Outlaw Motor Cycle Gangs*. Almost overnight, the Angels became a role model for "outlaw" groups across the globe.

According to many observers, such groups revelled in their new-found celebrity status and, in living up to their reputation, became even more shocking and antisocial than before. Inevitably, bikers in general and Harley-Davidson riders in particular were tarred with the same unsavoury brush. Some stereotypes persist, but the bad old days of

negative biker images have largely passed. In the United States, Harley owners have been growing older, wealthier and better educated. In 1984, the average age of a Harley buyer was 34; today it is almost 40, around one third of whom enjoyed a college education. Indeed, the modern stereotype is more of the well-off professional cruising any city's more fashionable streets rather than the grime-ridden outlaw of the past.

These days Harleys are the weekend wheels of lawyers, mayors and bankers: respectability, with an edge. This is all in motorcycle manufacturers' interests, for minority groups,

■ ABOVE *The original Hell's Angels were a group of Californian war veterans. Note Willie G., standing, facing the camera, third from the left.*

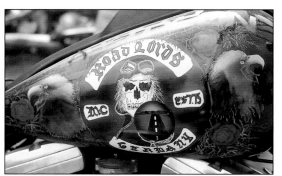

■ FAR LEFT *Imitators of the original Angels have since evolved as far apart as New Zealand...*

■ LEFT *...and Germany.*

■ RIGHT *Although "Hell's Angels" has become a cliche, Satan's Slaves is another well-known group of affiliated biker gangs.*

apart from tarring the rest, inevitably buy in minority numbers. One of the secondary purposes of HOG – the factory-sponsored Harley Owners' Group – was to broaden both the marque's appeal and its respectability, a service from which all bike producers benefit.

Hell's Angels and other so-called "outlaw" groups survive, and occasionally their activities hit the headlines. Perhaps the most notorious was a wave of knifings, bombings and shootings between rival Canadian gangs in the early 1990s, which left around 40 dead yet only attracted serious police attention when an

innocent bystander became a victim. In the late 1970s, Australia was the scene of a shoot-out in a supermarket parking lot between rival gangs. More recently, Denmark witnessed a spate of murders and even anti-tank missile attacks arising from a long-standing feud between the Angels and Bandidos for control of drugs interests. Crime – particularly the sale of stolen goods – and later the manufacture and dealing of hard drugs has long been a source of income for some outlaw bands which, in Europe in particular, are also associated with neo-Nazi activities. Even the FBI has shown an

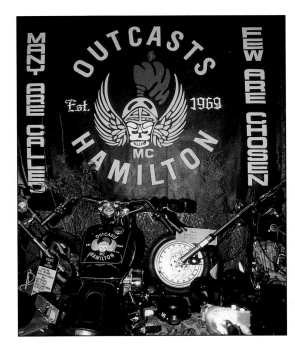

■ RIGHT *"Many are called... few are chosen" and even fewer care.*

■ FAR RIGHT *Sometimes known as "One Per Centers", although this veteran Angel begs to differ.*

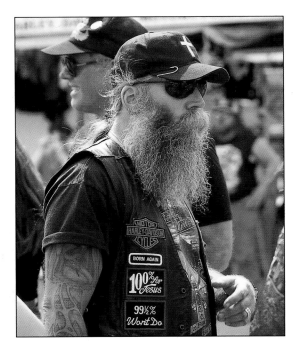

A DAY OF INFAMY

One of the most notorious episodes in American motorcycling history concerned the so-called Hollister riots of 1947. Events unfolded around the first Hollister Memorial Day races to be held since the Second World War, a focal point for recently demobbed biking GIs. As with the Isle of Man Tourist Trophy ("TT") today, the races were welcomed by residents of the little Californian town for the business and prosperity they brought.

Thousands arrived for the races, including bike clubs such as the "Booze Fighters" from Los Angeles and San Francisco. Main Street was crowded "like sardines" and undoubtedly rowdy. The press loved it: "Riots... Cyclists Take Over Town" and "Havoc in Hollister" cried the *San Francisco Chronicle*. Other papers and magazines quickly jumped on to exploit the bandwagon. Six years later, the "riots" would be commemorated on celluloid in

the film *The Wild One*, starring Marlon Brando and Lee Marvin. In the film, Johnny – angrily and effectively played by Brando – is asked what it is he's rebelling against. "Whaddya got?" he replies, one of Hollywood's most memorable lines. Although Harley-Davidsons feature heavily in the film, Brando is actually portrayed riding a Triumph. Nonetheless, the American Motorcycle Association saw fit to picket the movie on its release.

It was one thing for the movie to portray fiction, quite another for the contemporary press to do the same. For the truth was that the Hollister riots were largely fabricated. Some people were arrested for drunkenness but this was certainly nothing resembling a riot. As local hotelier Catherine Dabo later recalled to journalist Mark Gardiner, "I didn't even know anything had happened until I read the San Francisco papers."

Other Hollister residents were equally baffled: "It was a mess but there was no real evidence of physical damage," said Harry Hill, of the American Air Force.

"I brought my two daughters along... it never occurred to me to be worried about their safety," remembered local pharmacist Marylou Williams.

Finally and perhaps more to the point was the observation made by car mechanic Bert Lanning: "Some people don't like motorcycles, I guess."

According to one witness, cinema projectionist Gus Deserpa, a famous *Life* magazine photograph of a drunken biker sitting on his Harley surrounded by bottles, was faked. The drunk was real but it wasn't even his bike and the bottles had been gathered expressly to "improve" the picture.

Yes, Hollister was a weekend of infamy: for the media.

avid interest in them and certainly not because the G-men have an innate love of motorcycling. These self-styled "One Percenters" mostly exist on the fringes of Harley-Davidson culture and of motorcycling in general. Ironically, much of HOG's paraphernalia – its insignia, colours and organisation into "chapters" – echoes the ways of the outlaw gangs. Beards, badges and leather are part of many everyday Harley riders' uniforms but the trappings don't always say much about the person underneath. Sometimes the individual in the street must be hard-pressed to tell the difference. Perhaps Milwaukee likes it that way.

■ LEFT *These guys are probably discussing needlework.*

HARLEY AND ITS PUBLIC

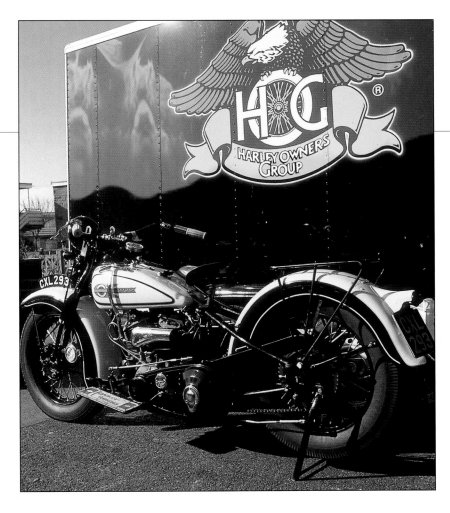

Harley-Davidson has a long and imaginative tradition of embracing the interests of its customers. As early as 1916, Juneau Avenue was producing its own magazine, *The Enthusiast*, to encourage pride of ownership and fellowship among Harley owners – and to do no harm to sales. Within three years, sales of the nickel magazine had reached 50,000. A trade equivalent, *Dealer News*, began in 1912 and a Spanish-language manual and catalogue, *Los Entusiastas Latinos*, appeared briefly the following year. *The Enthusiast* carried tales of racing, travels and other daring Harley deeds.

In the dark days of the 1930s Depression, the Harley "medal system" was born in which bonuses were offered to owners generating a motorcycle sale. January 1951 brought the Harley-Davidson Mileage Club which offered recognition for riding achievements. Harley riders could earn a pin badge and membership card for clocking up 25,000, 50,000 and 100,000 miles. By the end of 1954, no fewer than 73 Mileage Club members had logged 100,000 miles (160,930 kilometres).

The same concept of customer involvement – and a certain degree of desperation – lay behind the creation of the Harley Owners' Group (HOG). It was founded in 1983 (a year after Carl Wick's less phonetic HDOA – the Harley-Davidson Owners' Association).

Today, HOG is run by its own vice president (Bill, son of Willie G. Davidson). Under the factory's guidance and auspices, many Harley dealerships worldwide now run HOG groups, arranging everything from hog roasts to ride-aways, dances and charity events.

With the creation of HOG it was no longer enough to sell a customer a motorcycle – dealers had to be able to offer the lifestyle to go with it. A shrewd and prescient move, it

■ ABOVE *Years of effort and imagination have made HOG the envy of other manufacturers.*

■ BELOW *You need long sleeves to be a lifetime HOG devotee.*

anticipated the way motorcycling was going before any other manufacturer really took note. HOG now boasts more than 450,000 members in over 1,000 local chapters world-wide and has its own website, www.hog.com. On almost any summer weekend, it offers a choice of half a dozen rallies in the United States – plus others as far flung as Tunis, Darwin or Argentina. Like the motorcycles themselves, it is often imitated but never equalled.

If this portrays the company as only interested in the bottom line, it is also true that many of Harley's employees – at every level – are also committed motorcyclists. Harley-Davidson is fiercely protective of its interests, but also seeks to understand its customers. As the official company policy statement suggests: "It's one thing to have people buy your products. It's another for them to tattoo your name on their bodies." Sentiments such as that have brought Harley-Davidson a very long way.

CRUISING

Harley-Davidsons may be sold, cherished and owned in every corner of the globe but there isn't a hogger alive who doesn't fantasize about cruising a Hog across the good ol' US of A. Epic American journeys are the stuff of Milwaukee dreams: thundering across the wide-open Midwest prairies or the baking deserts of Utah and the south-west; soaring over the Rocky Mountains or gliding down California's coast-hugging Highway 1. There is simply nowhere else where Harleys feel so resolutely, resoundingly right.

Harleys suit the United States perfectly because they're part of the cultural landscape you find yourself riding through. In the United States, Harleys open doors, start conversations and bring smiles to passing faces, but best of all is the way they glide over the staggering panoply of scenery that is the American West.

■ CRUISING

From the saddle of an ElectraGlide or Low Rider, America passes by at a pace your senses can get a hook on; horizons rise in waves, roll

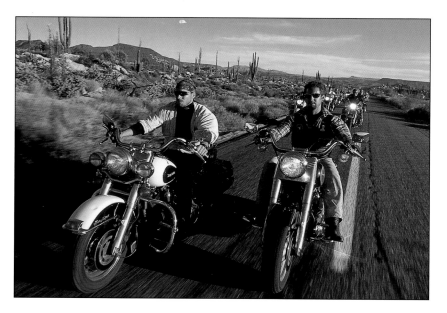

■ ABOVE *The author heading north on Route 95 in Utah, with the Colorado River in the background.*

■ LEFT *Dream come true: a group on a Harley package tour cruises through Baja, Mexico.*

■ OPPOSITE LEFT *What Hogs do best: thundering towards distant horizons in the American south-west.*

■ OPPOSITE RIGHT *A Fat Boy swings through the bends under the towering cliffs of Zion National Park, Utah, USA.*

■ **LEFT** *A group of German riders on hired Harleys near Monument Valley on the Arizona/Utah border.*

different: Arches, Canyonlands, Bryce, Capitol Reef and glorious Zion, to name but a few. Next door to Utah are Arizona and the Grand Canyon, Colorado and the Rockies, Nevada's sweeping high desert basins and the red rocks and white sands of New Mexico.

From magical, mystical Moab, it's just a short ride up Highway 191 to Canyonlands. Hang a left and let the Harley thunder up the

in like a gentle swell and gently recede under your wheels. It demands a different sort of tempo – more relaxed, less preoccupied with destinations – than riding in Europe. As it thumps over hills and plains, the big, lazy V-twin engine seems attuned to the environment in a way that other machines never could be. Then, with a jolt, you encounter somewhere like Utah – scenic America at its most extraordinary.

Utah is Mother Nature under hallucinogenic influence. Utah has National Parks in profusion, all with something spectacular and

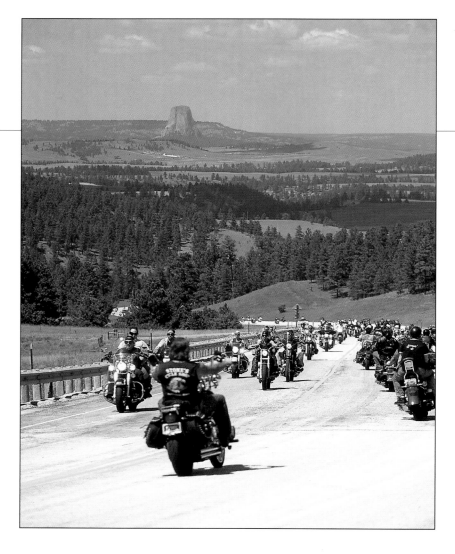

■ LEFT *Hoggers on a traditional ride-out from the Sturgis Rally to Dakota's Devil's Tower.*

■ BELOW *Baja California, the sea of Cortez beyond, and what better way to enjoy them?*

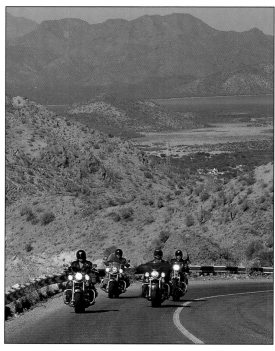

endless grades until suddenly the road stops and the world simply disappears. Gone. In its place, space – a void as big as the Alps. Half a mile (800 metres) below, the Colorado River surges noiselessly, framed by a rocky never-never-land that might be awe-inspiring if it were real. It takes a while to get your head around the fact that it is.

There's more. There always is in Utah. Shafer Canyon, Grand View Point, and then the daddy of them all, the Green River Overlook on the "Island in the Sky". From here, the western horizon is 100 miles (160km) away, about the distance from London to Bristol. Around where Berkshire ought to be is the baking wilderness of the Soda Springs Basin, through which Stillwater Canyon carves a distant trench which looks tiny but is fully 1,000ft (300 metres) deep. But for the shadows of passing clouds,

■ BELOW *108°F (42°C) in the shade, and there is no shade. Must be time for a cold beer.*

creeping as though in awe of the landscape, it could be the dark side of the Moon.

If the landscape is dramatic, the sheer scale is extraordinary. Take Route 41 – cresting a rise north of Montezuma Creek,

■ LEFT *Dead Horse Point, near Moab, just one of the scenic jewels of dazzling Utah.*

a view 200 miles (320 km) leaps into sight. Seventy-five miles (120km) away in Arizona, the orange spires of Monument Valley guard the western horizon; to the east, the snow-capped Colorado Rockies are fully 125 miles (200 km) distant. This a scene that is far larger than many countries in Europe, and yet it's a single, sweeping view – or a panoramic day's ride on a Harley-Davidson. For the great, mythic emptiness of the United States, nothing else comes close to experiencing it all – and more – as from the seat of a Harley-Davidson V-twin that has been made in Milwaukee.

■ BELOW *This man emigrated to the United States just to be able to do this.*

The Custom Scene

The identity of the first Harley-Davidson custom isn't recorded but it's surely almost as old as the company itself. It's in the nature of motorcycles that owners seek to "improve" them – not because there's necessarily anything wrong with the way they came out of the crate, but to add that extra touch of individuality.

Over the years, this "extra touch" turned from a trend into a craze and finally into a phenomenon. Today you'd be hard-pressed to find a Harley that has not been altered in some manner from the original that Milwaukee intended. Indeed, to judge by the amount of customizing that goes on, a Harley certainly isn't finished when it leaves the factory, if ever. Far from being discouraged by this slight on its judgement, the company actively encourages it. It's no coincidence that Harley-Davidson produces three catalogues crammed full of official "goodies", while the bikes themselves warrant only one. Custom Hogs are booming.

CUSTOM HARLEYS

A customized Harley today can be anything from a Sportster pared down to the barest essentials to a Glide decked out with almost anything you'd expect to find in a deluxe motorhome. Perhaps in the very early days, changes were functional: one carburettor worked better than another, this mudguard kept you cleaner than that. And, since America fell in love with horsepower almost as soon as there was such a thing, engine tuning quickly became a growth industry: in almost every state of the union, someone was willing to sell you high-lift camshafts, high-compression pistons or any of the other goodies that make an engine even stronger. In the racing field in particular, many tuners became legends for their prowess at extracting more power.

Extravagant cosmetic "tuning" came later. More than with any other make of motorcycle, Harley-Davidson customizing is an oddly circular process. First came Harley-Davidsons, which owners either lived with as they stood or adjusted to their tastes. Many of these creations were attractive in the extreme, a fact that was not lost on the people back at base in Milwaukee. Styling ideas which had first

■ ABOVE *Not surprisingly, this one goes by the name of "Full Metal Jacket".*

■ LEFT *This level of detail can take months to achieve.*

appeared as owners' one-offs fed back into the melting pot of Juneau Avenue design. Eventually, the wheel came full circle as the echoes reverberated through standard "factory custom" machines, beginning in 1970 with the FX1200 SuperGlide – although, at the time, the FX was resented by many in the custom scene for doing their job for them. Let's not forget that Buells – now an integral part of the Milwaukee range – began life as specials.

As far as graphics and paint are concerned, the inspiration reaches back farther still, to the art-deco designs with which the company

■ ABOVE *Custom can be three wheels...*

■ ABOVE RIGHT *...or designer grunge!*

attempted to sell bikes during the hardships of the 1930s. At the time, Harley was already marketing aftermarket parts such as mirrors and racks, but most were more functional than decorative. The true custom scene arrived in the California of the 1950s, with men such as Von Dutch and Ed Roth prominent. Often, 1930s art-deco was their inspiration in creating "blend" bikes – machines built from parts of several different models, as well as one-off components. Today, stylistic cues sometimes come from the Harley-Davidsons of the past, as demonstrated by the whole concept of "Retro-

Tech". Harley brochures today speak about machines of the 1950s inspiring several of their Softail models, although the Springer looks more like a child of the 1940s.

The 1960s and 1970s, of course, were the heyday of the chopper, with its radically extended forks, limited lock and lousy handling. These days, customizers and riders alike look for either something more functional or something that is very much more art than motorcycle – such as the creations of the doyen of customizers, Arlen Ness. Other celebrated custom artists include Dave Perewitz, Ricki

■ RIGHT *Presence, yes, but if you want ground clearance and rear suspension, look elsewhere.*

■ RIGHT
*Sometimes
practicality
comes a very
poor second
to effect.*

Battistini and Donnie Smith, but almost anyone with a Hog can join the scene in their own small way.

Mechanically as well as cosmetically, Harley-Davidson gladly promotes change, chiefly through its range of "Screaming Eagle" accessories, and they tacitly acknowledge that, even at 1450cc, the new Twin Cam engine can be further enhanced with a factory kit, increasing displacement to a mammoth 1550cc. Other suppliers, such as California's Custom Chrome, feed the fertile ground of Harley customs.

■ **ARLEN NESS**
The most revered of all Harley special builders is Arlen Ness, a slight, grey-haired Californian who doesn't so much customize Harleys as transform them into works of rolling art. Like so many others in the custom field, Arlen Ness' interest started as a hobby, growing and growing as people took note of his creations and begged him to craft something equally extraordinary for them.

Beginning with a 1937 Knucklehead bought for $300 in 1967, he now designs and manufactures everything from the tiniest, most exquisite chrome-plated detail to his own overhead-cam "Harley" twin, the engine that powers the gleaming Light-Ness machine. "I started out painting motorcycles in my

garage," he explains, "but it got so busy with people coming and going that I couldn't get any work done, so I ended up renting a little store. This meant people would go there instead so I could work at home in the daytime and kept the shop open at night."

From paint jobs and custom handlebars, he now runs a huge mail-order business from a 70,000sq ft (6,500sq metre) building in San Francisco's Bay area. He actually builds just a handful of specials each year, at prices ranging from $25,000 to $50,000, but turns away far more customers than that. Sometimes the problem is sheer pressure of work (would "Busy-Ness" make a good project?), sometimes it's aesthetic.

■ ABOVE *"Choppers"
like this are now passé
in the US, but live on in
parts of Europe.*

■ BELOW *Sometimes,
Milwaukee must wonder
why it bothers at all.*

■ LEFT *Light-Ness (closest), Antique-Ness and Smooth-Ness, three of Arlen Ness' most famous creations.*

■ BELOW *Arlen Ness (left) with Hank, president of the Chopper Club.*

"We turn away quite a few people if we don't like a style they want or if we don't think they would be real happy… and others can't seem to make up their mind," he explains.

"There isn't a lot of money in building bikes. I just do it for fun." Or maybe Arlen just hates the one he hasn't built yet: Idle-Ness.

■ **THE BIKES**

The silver machine – "Light-Ness" – is powered by Ness' 100-inch (1,639cc) ohc "lightweight" motor housed in a special aluminium frame. Following the same theme, tank, fenders, mufflers and most other components are also highly-polished aluminium. Arlen values the bike at some $40,000.

The yellow bike is "Antique-Ness", Ness' first sidecar outfit. Based around a 1200cc Harley Sportster engine, it was created over a period of nine months by Arlen and fellow American customizers, Mun and Jimmy Rose. Built for Ness' wife, Bev, it was styled along the lines (if not the colour) of Harleys of the

1920s. Similar machines can be bought in kit form for around $27,000.

Although to some eyes it resembles half of a 1959 Cadillac, "Smooth-Ness" was inspired by the sleek, flowing lines of a classic Bugatti motor car. The all-aluminium body houses a rubber-mounted Harley "Evo" V-twin in a prototype Softail-type chassis. It took a year to build and is valued at $100,000.

■ BELOW *An earlier and slightly less radical Ness special.*

Competition

Although Harley-Davidson is not always automatically associated with the white heat of competition, it is part of the deep-seated American tradition of racing pretty much anything on wheels. The first mention of a Harley racing dates from 1904. Perry Mack (possibly the company's first employee) set a speed record on a local Milwaukee track as early as 1905. The first recorded "factory" win in actual competition came in 1908, with Walter Davidson at the controls.

Company presidents don't figure among the results any more, but Harley-Davidson has won since on tarmac, dirt, boards, ice, grass and just about any other medium possible. Much of this success has been in the spectacular field of American dirt-track racing, 130mph (210kph) speedway, with huge fields of 16 riders competing like fury for millimetres of space. On the grand prix front, Harley's Italian connection Aermacchi brought Walter Villa four world crowns between 1974 and 1976. The factory has recently been striving towards a competitive presence in world superbike action with the VR1000 twin ridden by former AMA Number Ones Chris Carr and Thomas Wilson, and more recently by former World Superbike champion Scott Russell.

♨ RACING

Harley-Davidson's early years were marked by racing successes too numerous to mention. The earliest of note came in 1908 when one of the first V-twins, ridden by company president Walter Davidson claimed victory in the FAM (Federation of American Motorcyclists) seventh annual endurance event in New York's Catskill Mountains. The 365-mile (587km) course was dauntingly rugged, yet "so strong was my confidence," Davidson later said, "that I carried with me no additional parts." This was in marked contrast to several other manufacturers, whose machines were followed by car-loads of spares.

In July of the same year, the Chicago Motorcycle Club sponsored a hill climb in nearby Algonquin, Illinois. Fastest time of the day went to Harvey Bernard riding a Harley-Davidson. Mysteriously, contemporary photographs clearly show Bernard aboard a V-twin machine, yet the model did not officially appear until early the following year.

The succeeding years were distinguished by numerous, similar Harley-Davidson successes, yet they almost exclusively involved machines which were privately owned and run. A company advertisement from September 1911 bragged, "We don't believe in racing and we don't make a practice of it, but when Harley-Davidson owners with their own stock machines win hundreds of miles from the factory, we can't help crowing about it."

This boast was nowhere more graphically demonstrated than in the San José road race of 1912, in which a 61-inch Model X8E triumphed by the small matter of 17 miles

■ ABOVE *Harley-Davidsons board racing in Los Angeles, 1912.*

■ LEFT *Harley had major success in racing from the outset.*

(27 kilometres). That same year, Harley-Davidson twins won at Bakersfield and the following year took first, second and third place in a 225-mile (362km) dash from Harrisburg to Pennsylvania and back, but these were private machines contesting relatively obscure races.

In 1914 – four years after Indian had won the prestigious Isle of Man TT – Milwaukee bowed to the inevitable when Bill Harley established a works race department which was to continue its winning ways into the 1970s. Some reports refer to instant success in taking that year's Dodge City 300-mile (480km) race, when in fact only two Harleys finished, well off the pace, in a race dominated by Indian. Clearly, the battle-hardened Springfield eight-valve twin was a formidable foe, but under the direction of the Bills Harley and Ottaway, Harley's progress was rapid. By 1915, Milwaukee twins were the bikes to beat.

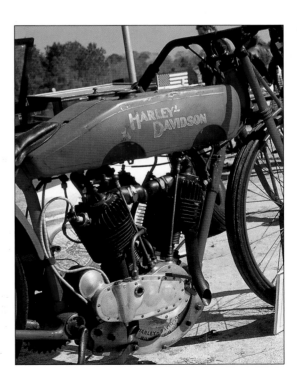

■ ABOVE *One of the legendary "Peashooter" racers of the 1920s, in this case prepared for hill-climbing.*

■ BELOW RIGHT *From 1920, a board-track racer.*

The step from factory racers to racer production was a short and logical one. By 1916, $250 would buy any aspiring racer a special stripped-down competition version of the Harley twin, producing 11 horsepower and capable of around 75mph (120kph).

As well as speed, Harley iron chased many endurance records during the same period. In 1917, a Harley-Davidson ridden by Alan Bedell covered 1,000 miles (1,610km) non-stop at Ascot Park, taking almost 21 hours and averaging a remarkable 48.3mph (77.7kph).

In the same year, another Harley set a similar mark fitted with a sidecar.

RACE BOSSES

It's a remarkable fact that, once it finally got around to racing officially, Harley-Davidson needed a mere three race-team managers in all its many decades of competition – Bill Ottaway, Hank Syvertson and Dick O'Brien. They, too, became legends.

The factory crew's early successes were overseen by the cool gaze of Bill Ottaway. Described as "a wizard" by William Davidson, Ottaway began his career at Thor, manufacturer of proprietary motorcycle engines, leaving for Juneau Avenue in 1913. A talented engineer and a shrewd manager, he saw the factory squad through its formative years and into the glory days of the 1920s before

Hank Syvertson took over as director of racing.

Dick O'Brien began a lifetime of working on Harley engines at Puckett's in Orlando, Florida. Apart from a period of military service as a senior aircraft mechanic during the Second World War, he continued as a Harley service-shop manager, with a special talent for tuning racing machines – Daytona Speedway was, after all, only a couple of hours distant. In June 1957, he joined the factory race squad as Syvertson's assistant. Three months later Syvertson retired and O'Brien took the helm, a position he held until his retirement in 1983.

■ LEFT *Wrecking Crew at Dodge City in 1920. From left: race boss Bill Ottaway, Maldwyn Jones, Ralph Hepburn, Fred Ludlow, Otto Walker, Ray Weishaar, Jim Davis and mechanic Hank Syvertsen.*

■ **THE WRECKING CREW**

During the buoyant 1920s, Harley-Davidson's competitive exploits were even more remarkable than the salvos of new models roaring out of Milwaukee. In 1920, a Harley became the first powered vehicle to top California's 10,000ft (3,050 metre) "Old Baldy" hill-climb. In February 1921, at Fresno, a Harley became the first bike to win a race at an average of more than 100mph (160kph).

Many of the factory's innumerable successes came courtesy of the legendary Harley-Davidson "Wrecking Crew". The Crew was almost unbeatable on the dirt and boards of America from the days before the First World War until the factory briefly pulled out of racing following the 1920 slump. Board racing, on banked ovals of raw wood, was uniquely – and spectacularly – American.

The Crew included barnstorming individuals: Eddie Brinck, Otto Walker, Jim Davis, Leslie "Red" Parkhurst and many more. Walker marked the factory's withdrawal by taking a 61cu in, eight-valve machine to victory in a 50-mile (80km) race at San Joaquin, California, at the sensational average

speed of 101.43mph (163.23kph). The crew began 1920 by taking the first four places in the Ascot 100-miler (160.93km) race on America's fastest track. In February, Harleys set 23 records, including four by Parker at the kilometre, mile – both at more than 103mph (165kph) – two mile and five mile marks.

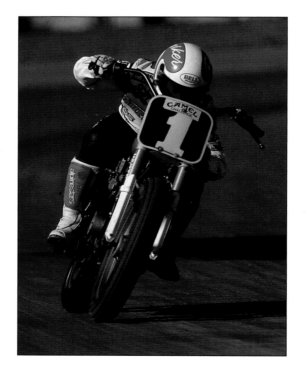

■ LEFT *Scott Parker, the most successful dirt-track rider in AMA history.*

These men, riding in little more than cloth caps, sweatshirts and jodhpurs, were tough little heroes in the same mould that was later to produce stars such as Cal Rayborn, Jay Springsteen and Scott Parker. The racing life was hard and cruel. Eddie Brinck himself was killed when a tyre blew out in a race at Springfield, Massachusetts.

As America's road system developed, it was only natural that men would create some form of contest on it. As early as 1920, Hap Sherer took a Sport Twin (584cc boxer) from Denver to Chicago in 48 hours – no easy feat even today. Meanwhile, Walter Hadfield made a habit of lowering the "Three Flags Run" record from Vancouver (Canada) to Tijuana (Mexico), a route on which Fred Deeley later averaged more than 104mpg (36km/litre). Perhaps most impressive of all was the remarkable Earl Hadfield, who covered more than 3,000-plus miles (4,800-plus km) between New York and Los Angeles in less than 78 hours. At around the same time, the immortal Windy Lindstrom was king of America's booming hill-climb scene, on specially-modified Milwaukee iron.

Harley victories were by no means confined to the United States. Harley-Davidson found willing, winning pilots as far apart as Scandinavia and Australia, notching up successes in fields as diverse as ice speedway and grass track. At the legendary banked

■ ABOVE *The legendary Cal Rayborn on the XR750, Brands Hatch, 1972.*

■ BELOW *Jay Springsteen is one in a long line of champions that stem from the legacy of the Wrecking Crew of the early part of the 20th century.*

Brooklands track in Surrey, England, Doug Davidson (no relation) took a factory 1000cc ioe twin to a record-breaking average of 100.76mph (162.15kph) over a flying kilometre. Within a few months, a similar machine ridden by Claude Temple had taken records in the hour, five mile, flying mile and kilometre.

Yet even these efforts paled when compared to those of the mercurial Englishman, Freddy Dixon, riding a special twin with four pipes and eight overhead valves. Dixon was nearly unbeatable in all forms of competition from hill-climbs to long-distance events around the daunting Brooklands circuit. On 9 September 1923 at Arpajon, near Paris, Dixon set a new world speed mark of 106.8mph/171.8kph (a record Harley-Davidson would not hold again until 1970). Ten months later he was at it again, flying through the half-mile at the Clipstone Speed Trials at 103.44mph (166.47kph). In 1925 he averaged 100.1mph (161kph) winning the Brooklands 1000cc championship – possibly the noisiest victory ever, for the machine had no exhaust pipes.

■ LEFT *The Knucklehead streamliner on which Joe Petrali set record speeds at Florida's Daytona Beach.*

■ JOE PETRALI

If Freddy Dixon had a counterpart on Harley's home turf, it was surely the legendary Joe Petrali. More than perhaps any other man, Petrali single-handedly made Harley-Davidson an unbeatable force during the late 1920s and throughout the 1930s. Born in Sacramento, California in 1904, he owned his first bike at 13 years of age and was racing – and winning – on boards by the time he was 16. Petrali first hit the big time when he showed up bike-less at Altoona, Pennsylvania, in 1925. Luckily for him, former Wrecking Crew man Ralph Hepburn had broken a hand. Petrali took over the factory Harley-Davidson instead. He was practically unknown at the time.

Less than an hour later (59 minutes and 47.2 seconds later to be exact), Petrali was a legend. He left the entire field of hardened pros in a cloud of dust, averaging 100.32mph (161.45kph) in the 100-mile (160.93-km) race over Altoona's lightning-fast boards. Earlier that same day, Jim Davis won the five-mile "sprint" at over 110mph (177kph) – at a time when the Indianapolis car race was being won at less than 101mph (163kph). From then on, there was no stopping Joe Petrali. He became so dominant that, for more than a decade, the rest were effectively riding for second place. In 1935, he won every single event of the National season, including five wins in a single

day at Syracuse, New York. In 1937, he took a Knucklehead streamliner through the timing strip on the sands of Daytona Beach at 136.183mph (219.159kph), a record that still stands.

■ THE MICHIGAN MEN

Flint, Michigan, must be a remarkable place. Jay Springsteen is from Flint, where they build Chevrolets out of the same hard stuff. So is Scott Parker. So, too, is "Black" Bart Markel.

■ BELOW *Scott Parker rockets the XR750 around the Del Mar track.*

During a dirt-track career that began in 1957 and spanned 23 years, Markel was the original Michigan hard man. He won three national titles (in 1962, 1965 and 1966) but it was his style that caught the eye. Old boys still whistle in awe at the memory of Markel bouncing off guard rails, bales and other bikes – whatever it would take him to get to the finish line first.

Like the rest, he had to race on tarmac as well as dirt to take those titles. He crashed an awful lot, for the simple reason that "he

■ ABOVE LEFT *Scott Parker (left) and Jay Springsteen (right), both chips off the same Flint block.*

■ ABOVE RIGHT *During the 1950s, the flathead KRTT needed a capacity edge to compete with European ohv twins.*

■ BELOW *As well as his prowess on dirt, Springsteen was an able road racer, as here with the Sundance twin.*

refused to slow down for the turns," according to Harley-Davidson race boss Dick O'Brien. Instead, he just threw the bike sideways and slid round the turn – or slid off.

For the past decade and perhaps for all time, Parker has been "The Man" on the ovals, picking up titles most years and smashing every record in the books. Like his buddy Jay Springsteen (who was champion from 1976 to 1978), he's also from Flint, Michigan.

Born in 1962, Parker started riding at the age of six and racing at 13. He picked up his first Number One plate in 1988, posting four consecutive titles before Harley-Davidson team-mate Chris Carr took the crown in 1992. Ricky Graham won in 1993, but Parker struck back with five consecutive crowns since. His nine titles make him far and away the most successful rider in AMA dirt-track history.

THE HOLE IN THE WALL GANG

In the Depression years of the 1930s, people would try almost anything to turn a buck. If Evel Knievel enlivened the 1970s, the 1930s shone for an assorted bunch of desperadoes who might be called the "Hole in the Wall Gang". These weren't Butch and Sundance but a fellowship of maniacs who believed that if you hurtled a bike fast enough at a solid timber wall, you could punch clean through it. The first recorded case of a Harley-Davidson attempting the stunt came in Texas in 1932 when Daisy May Hendrich thudded repeatedly through inch-thick boards. (Daisy May, incidentally, was a man.) J.R. Bruce of Wooster, Ohio, went one better by setting the wall ablaze before the stunt. Wall stunts, burning or not, were a common feature of American county fairs in the 1930s.

■ RIGHT *Quarter-mile action at Daytona. The bikes are Rotax-engined single-cylinder "Harleys".*

■ DIRT TRACK

Dirt track "oval" racing spans the decades and is the essence of American motorcycle sport. This is the craziest and meanest of them all – chasing the prized "Number One" plate of the AMA champion. Although superficially similar to speedway, oval racing is held on tracks a mile or half-mile long where 750cc machines reach speeds in excess of 130mph(210kph).

Dirt track grew up on the county fairgrounds of middle America, a sort of rodeo on two wheels. In the early years, it was barely organized and, even during times when it was, it often wasn't: an "outlaw" series flourished in the 1940s. In 1946, the AMA founded the national championship which has been keenly contested ever since.

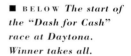

■ LEFT *Scott Parker leads the field into turn one during the Sacramento Mile.*

■ BELOW *The start of the "Dash for Cash" race at Daytona. Winner takes all.*

quarter-, half- and mile flat-track racing, TT Steeplechase (a cross between dirt track and motocross) and European-style road-racing. These days, there's a separate road-race series, and the days of the great all-rounders are over – Bubba Shobert was the last, with three consecutive AMA titles. Shobert held the record for mile wins with 25, until eclipsed by current champ Scott Parker in 1991. The famed Harley-Davidson "Number One" logo, incidentally, was designed in 1970 to celebrate Mert Lawwill's AMA Grand National title.

The pre-eminence of Americans in 500 road-racing grands prix has been ascribed to the special skills honed by dirt-track experience. Champion riders, including the likes of Kenny Roberts, Wayne Rainey, Eddie Lawson and most of the rest cut their teeth learning how to control bucking, sliding motorcycles on dirt.

The early Harley-Davidson heroes were men like Jimmy Chann, Joe Leonard and Carroll Resweber, who took ten titles between them from 1947 to 1961. In those days and until 1986, the champion's cherished "Number One" was decided in a series which included

Done well – and the top exponents do it very well – dirt track is oddly balletic, almost poetry on wheels. But it can go wrong with sickening suddenness, ending in a maelstrom of muck, blood and machinery. Catch the motorcycle film *On Any Sunday* and you'll see men thrown through four-inch fence posts, clamber to their feet, dust off the dirt and the straw and climb right back on their bikes. You'll see men who can't walk drifting both wheels at three figure speeds. You'll see Dick Mann saw off a plaster cast – "I'm a fast healer" – just to chase that Number One plate.

■ ABOVE *What it's all about: the coveted Number One plate.*

■ BELOW *The all-conquering XR750, brutal and elegant at the same time.*

■ ABOVE *Springsteen's XR750, sponsored by Bartels of California.*

DRAG RACING

If all Harley-Davidsons thunder, none thunder with quite such a clap as fire-breathing drag machines. Like so much else in motorcycle sport, drag racing lies deep in the soul of America. Naturally, Harley-Davidsons have always been there when the lights go out at the start of the quarter mile. Men like Marion Owens, Leo Payne and Danny Johnson, with his celebrated double-engine Harley, continued to show that big-twin power was a force to be reckoned with long after multi-cylinder machines and two-strokes had dominated in other fields.

■ ABOVE, LEFT AND RIGHT *The idea is to expend as much money and effort in the shortest possible time. Strange, but thousands are addicted to this power-mad sport.*

■ CAL RAYBORN

The great Cal Rayborn never won the coveted Number One plate but that didn't stop him being the best. Rayborn was the consummate road racer, a true natural and arguably the man who opened the door to Kenny Roberts, Wayne Rainey and other Americans who have since made their mark in grand prix competition. From Spring Valley, California, Rayborn won Daytona twice, as well as nine other major AMA road-race wins. Yet his career almost never began at all – in 1958, at only 18 years of age, he broke his back at California's Riverside circuit.

Never truly at home on dirt, Rayborn compensated with absolute mastery on tarmac. In 1968, he became the first man to average 100mph (160.93kph) winning the then world-renowned Daytona 200-miler (321.86km) – and comfortably: he recorded 101.29mph (163kph). In the process, his XR750 Harley-Davidson lapped the entire field. He won again in 1969, in what would prove to be the last Daytona triumph for Milwaukee. British fans will remember him for trouncing the field in the Easter Match Races in 1972, also on a factory XR750. The big V-twin had almost

■ BELOW *The late, great Cal Rayborn pictured at Oulton Park, England, at the Easter Match Races, 1972.*

■ ABOVE *Evel Knievel, the ultimate showman – especially for Milwaukee. The tank says "Harley-Davidson" but the engine's a Triumph twin.*

been dismissed in favour of factory Triumphs, Nortons and Japanese machines, but Rayborn made them eat their words.

Rayborn also found time for a succession of speed record attempts, in his case on Utah's Bonneville salt flats. In 1970, he took a pencil-thin, 19ft (6-metre), streamlined 1480cc Sportster to a staggering 254.84mph (410.11kph), a figure he later improved to 265.49mph (427.25kph).

Rayborn was killed tragically in 1973 while riding in Australia, ironically on a two-stroke which seized and threw him into a trackside barrier.

■ EVEL KNIEVEL

If Harley-Davidson's earlier successes had been in racing, Evel Knievel had a better idea: he'd make them fly. A pure showman, Knievel chased women and long-jump records in roughly equal measure. Beginning in 1970, his crazy schemes ran on Harley-Davidson power, mainly with a succession of XR750 machines.

Knievel's bikes had to be tough – if not quite as tough as the man himself. He jumped cars (21 at Ontario Speedway on 28 February 1971), trucks, buses and even the fountain at Caesar's Palace in Las Vegas. Evel's problem was that he was effectively on piece-rate – his fees rose with the number of obstacles cleared. And he liked money: the jumps got bigger and the litany of crashes grew longer. In the process, he broke most of his important bones and a lot of smaller ones. When you went to watch Evel Knievel, you knew that you were in for a show. The Las Vegas leap resulted in one of his more spectacular crashes when he

■ RIGHT *The Sport-engined streamliner which took the 250cc land speed record in 1965, driven by George Roeder, pictured here.*

■ FAR RIGHT *Here the Knievel flying machine is pictured astride the genuine Harley article.*

bounced off cars, cartwheeling through the Caesar's Palace parking lot.

By 1978, Knievel had run out of conventional things to jump and crash into, and announced he would leap the Grand Canyon instead. The Canyon is over a mile wide and almost as deep, so the local Native American tribe probably did him a favour when they vetoed the plan. Undeterred, Knievel turned his sights to the Snake River Canyon, abandoning his beloved Harley-Davidson for a rocket-powered projectile. However, the rocket only fizzed, and the attempt was a failure.

In 1999, Knievel's son put the record straight when he, finally and triumphantly, leapt over the Grand Canyon.

■ GRANDS PRIX

Whatever disappointments the arrangement brought in terms of sales, Harley's ties to Aermacchi produced resounding success on the world stage during the mid-1970s. Factory RR-250 and RR-350 twins ridden by Italy's Walter Villa won three consecutive 250cc world titles and one 350cc title between 1974 and 1976.

Producing 58bhp at 12,000rpm and 70bhp at 11,400rpm respectively, these were unlike traditional Harley-Davidson twins.

The engines were two-stroke, initially air-cooled but later with full liquid cooling. The gearboxes housed six ratios, due to the RR's narrow, peaky powerband. These two-stroke

■ ABOVE LEFT *Based on the XR1000 roadster engine, Lucifer's Hammer surprised many onlookers by its speed in Battle of the Twins competition during the 1980s.*

■ ABOVE RIGHT *Walter Villa contesting the 250cc Belgian grand prix at Spa-Francorchamps in 1977 on an RR250. Despite carrying the number 10, he was world champion at the time.*

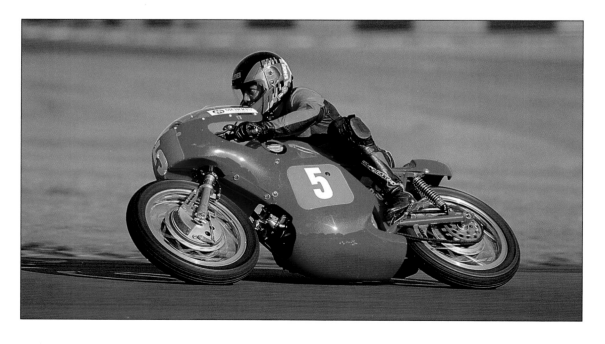

■ LEFT *An Aermacchi 350 charges round the Brands Hatch circuit.*

twins were also raced with some success
in the United States by championship-winning
riders such as Cal Rayborn and Gary Scott.

■ LUCIFER'S HAMMER

Perhaps the single most celebrated Harley
racer of recent times, Lucifer's Hammer began
its racing life with a win at Daytona in 1983
with the great Jay Springsteen on the saddle.
The same bike went on to dominate American
Battle of the Twins racing (under Harley
Owners' Group sponsorship) during much of
the 1980s, taking Gene Church to three
consecutive American titles.

Powered by a highly-tuned XR1000 engine
generating 104bhp at 7,000rpm, the Hammer
was timed at no less than 158mph (254kph) at
Daytona. The XR750 road race frame,
albeit heavily reworked, had debuted at
Daytona fully ten years before Springsteen's
epic win, showing that at Milwaukee, they
build 'em to last.

■ 883 SPORT TWINS SERIES

The Sport Twins series, launched in the United
States in 1989, quickly became a worldwide
phenomenon. A "one-make" competition for
modified 883cc Harley twins, the series'
instant success saw it exported to race tracks

■ ABOVE *A Harley
superbike – the factory
VR1000.*

■ ABOVE RIGHT
*Harley's inspired 883
Sportster series even
attracted stars such as
Jay Springsteen.*

■ BELOW *Using double
overhead cams in each
head, four valves per
cylinder and fuel
injection, the VR1000
is unlike any Harley
ever seen on the street.*

all around the world, where spectators would
flock to hear the thunder of a grid-full of
Milwaukee twins. When Harley created the
series, it probably expected it to be an all-
American affair. If so, they were mistaken. That
very first American Sports Twins series title
was won by an Englishman, Nigel Gale.

■ VR1000

The factory has recently been striving towards
a competitive presence in world superbike
action. This has been achieved with the
VR1000 twin ridden by former AMA Number
Ones Chris Carr and Thomas Wilson and,
latterly, by the former World Superbike
champion, Scott Russell.

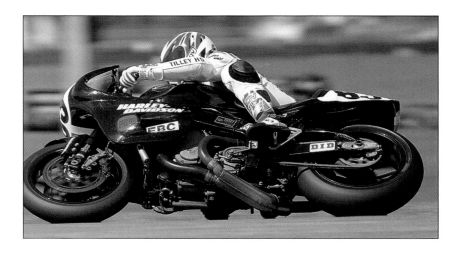

The Publishers would like to
thank the following for their kind
permission to reproduce their
photographs:

John Bolt
44tr, 45tr, 49b, 59br, 77b, 98 (all),
99tl/tr/br, 108–9, 110 (all), 111 (all),
112 (all), 113 (tr/b).

John Caroll
91b, 100t.

Alan Cathcart
126tl.

Bob Clarke
30m, 34t, 41tl, 43t, 60t, 87m/b, 94bl,
124ml.

Neil Dalleywater
43br, 74br.

Kobal
94t/m, 97tr, 125t/br.

Mac McDiarmid
8–9, 28t/b, 33, 35b, 41tr, 45b, 47tl/b,
49t, 60t/m/br, 61tr, 62 (all), 63tl/b,
64b, 65 (all), 66 (all), 67 (all),
71(all), 72t, 73br, 74t/bl, 76t, 78t, 82
(all), 83 (all), 84–5, 92–3, 95tl/bl/br,
101bl, 103b, 104 (all), 105 (all),
106tr/b, 107 (all), 113tl, 118bl, 120t,
121tl, 122 (all), 123m/br, 126b.

Don Morley
13br, 21b, 35t, 42b, 59tl, 126tr.

B. R. Nicholls
119t, 123b.

Quadrant
2.

Tony Stone
50–1.

Garry Stuart
11t/ml, 12tl/tr, 13bl, 14bl/br, 15t,
16t/bl, 18b, 19 (all), 20 (all), 21t,
22t/b, 23t, 24 (all), 25 (all), 26 (all),
27 (all), 29 (all), 30t/b, 31 (all), 32
(all), 34b, 36 (all), 37 (all), 38 (all),
39 (all), 40 (all), 41b, 42t, 43bl,
44t/b, 45tl, 46 (all), 47tr, 48 (all),
50tl/b, 58b, 60bl, 61tl/b, 68–9,
70(all), 72b, 73t/bl, 75 (all), 76b, 77t,
78b, 86br, 88 (all), 88tl/m, 90t/b, 91t,
96 (all), 97 (all), 102b, 106tl, 114–5,
117t/b, 119b, 120b, 121tr, 123t,
124t/mr, 127tr/b.

All other photographs courtesy
of Harley-Davidson, Inc.

t=top b=bottom l=left r=right
m=middle tr= top right tl=top left
ml=middle left mr=middle right
bl=bottom left br=bottom right
lm=left middle tmr=top middle
right tml=top middle left